Praise for *Do Something Beautiful*

In a world of despair, injustice, and hopelessness, Moore reminds us of the beauty of the cross and challenges us to reflect that beauty in our everyday lives and in our everyday relationships. *Do Something Beautiful* is a must-read guide to finding your place in God's story.

TOM LIN
President/CEO of InterVarsity Christian Fellowship

This book presents us with a beautifully framed call to live a beautiful and impactful life for Jesus. York brings a distinctly missional approach to abroad range of life's pursuits and interests, and he does it is a way that is eminently doable and deeply appealing. A worthy read.

ALAN HIRSCH
Founder of Forge International, 100 Movements,
and the 5Q Collective

In *Do Something Beautiful,* York Moore has both told his personal story while explaining "the story of everything". Moore not only helps us understand concepts from Scripture like righteousness, justice, beauty, and mercy, but helps us long to experience them and describes practical ways we share them with others.

STEVE DOUGLAS
President of Cru

In a world filled with noise, York Moore is a prophetic voice with a burning passion for Jesus, justice, and people. More than "another preacher," York has given his life to fight for the voiceless, marginalized, and build bridges to bring glimpses of God's Kingdom to earth. *Do Something Beautiful* is more than a book. It's an invitation into the story of God, who is making all things new. Spending time with York has enriched, and changed my life, and I believe this book can change yours to see a God who is bigger, better, and more beautiful than your wildest dreams. And the best part . . . He wants to use you! In a world full of division, pain, and brokenness, let's do something beautiful."

NICK HALL
Evangelist, Founder of PULSE and
CEO of the US Lausanne Committee

York's book *Do Something Beautiful* has been a joy to read! He offers great perspective for our current generation's longing to be a part of the bigger story. Using honest and transparent personal stories, York beautifully portrays the Gospel as the foundation to that inner longing for true beauty. Personally, I love how he did not try to avoid the pain in his own life or those around him, but rather embraced it in order to find God in the midst of pain-that we must be willing to embrace the cost, however high, to do something truly beautiful. The stories he tells will stir your heart to do something beautiful as you walk with Jesus! There is a longing for true revival and awakening all across the earth and its stories and books like these that will provide tools for how to walk in the radical love of Jesus and see revival and awakening!

LINDY AND THE CIRCUIT RIDERS

DO
SOMETHING
BEAUTIFUL

DO
SOMETHING
BEAUTIFUL

THE STORY OF
EVERYTHING AND
A GUIDE TO FINDING
YOUR PLACE
IN IT

R. YORK MOORE

MOODY PUBLISHERS
CHICAGO

Scriptures taken from the Holy Bible, New International Version®, NIV®. Copyright © 1973, 1978, 1984, 2011 by Biblica, Inc.™ Used by permission of Zondervan. All rights reserved worldwide. www.zondervan.com. The "NIV" and "New International Version" are trademarks registered in the United States Patent and Trademark Office by Biblica, Inc.™

Emphasis in Scripture has been added.

Some details have been changed to protect the privacy of individuals.

Edited by Randall Payleitner
Interior and cover design: Erik M. Peterson
Cover image of hot-air balloons copyright © 2016 by Tanachot / iStock (619250406). All rights reserved.

Library of Congress Cataloging-in-Publication Data

Names: Moore, R. York, 1969- author.
Title: Do something beautiful : the story of everything and a guide to
   finding your place in it / R. York Moore.
Description: Chicago : Moody Publishers, 2018. | Includes bibliographical
   references.
Identifiers: LCCN 2018010738 (print) | LCCN 2018023473 (ebook) | ISBN
   9780802496591 (ebook) | ISBN 9780802417121
Subjects: LCSH: Christian life.
Classification: LCC BV4501.3 (ebook) | LCC BV4501.3 .M66565 2018 (print) |
   DDC 248.4--dc23
LC record available at https://lccn.loc.gov/2018010738

ISBN: 978-0-8024-1712-1

We hope you enjoy this book from Moody Publishers.
Our goal is to provide high-quality, thought-provoking books
and products that connect truth to your real needs and
challenges. For more information on other books and
products written and produced from a biblical perspective,
go to www.moodypublishers.com or write to:

Moody Publishers
820 N. LaSalle Boulevard
Chicago, IL 60610

1 3 5 7 9 10 8 6 4 2

Printed in the United States of America

TO MY MOM, BECAUSE YOU
TAUGHT ME TO MARVEL AT
THE WORLD, TO FIND BEAUTY AND
PURSUE WHAT IS GOOD,
EVEN WHEN EVERYTHING
AROUND US WAS OTHERWISE.

CONTENTS

FOREWORD

Dr. Cornelius Plantinga, a great theologian and former president of Calvin Seminary, once wrote a book on sin titled *Not the Way It's Supposed to Be*. It's a powerful treatise on sin and shalom, and I cannot think of a better phrase to describe the visceral feeling that we find ourselves in as we navigate through this world we find ourselves in today.

As we look to the world around us, often dark, we discern that even a world that does not know the nuances of hamartiology (the study of sin) can feel the pangs of the world's brokenness, fracturing, and can identify that gut feeling of the loss of innocence. This brokenness is coming to the surface now more than ever, and our response to this brokenness is crucial. How Christians bring clarity in the midst of a world of confusion will determine much for the witness of Jesus in the world in our generation.

But there is much hope in the world. Roy Hession, in his work *We Would See Jesus*, says, "The glorious, central fact of Christianity is that God has made a full and final revelation of Himself in Jesus which has made Him understandable, accessible, and desirable to the simplest and most fearful of us."

This is infinitely attractive and profoundly glorious. We have access to this salvation in the midst of a world gone wrong and a universe gone sideways. And York Moore shows us the true solution that the narrative into healing, wholeness, and flourishing is found in the light of Jesus. Jesus' beautiful story encompasses and wraps up what we see in the world. Moore helps us get a glimpse of that light, that narrative, and that beauty that is pervading the world in opposition to the darkness.

Moore helps guide us to some of these healing paths through weaving in personal narrative, solid biblical wisdom, and pointing us to Jesus and His narrative that runs counterintuitive and countercultural to the world around us. It doesn't simply stay theoretical; Moore shows us how Jesus moves into the real world and connects us with one another as well. We need someone to adjust the lens on how we see brokenness properly framed with the beauty of Jesus and His mission for the world, and York Moore is the man for the job.

God's story is a world becoming right again, made whole by the One who lived, loved, died, and resurrected to bring us into a great exchange: our sin for His perfection, our brokenness for His wholeness, our death for His life. York Moore shows us that this message of a world becoming right again is the type of message that can shine like a firefly in a dark and despondent world that will one day be the way it's supposed to be.

ED STETZER
Billy Graham Distinguished Chair, Wheaton College

INTRODUCTION

Within every person is an undeniable longing we can never totally shake. This book is about that longing. I want to give names to the contours of it and why you feel it, and show you how that longing can begin to be satisfied through understanding your place in the story of everything. So, let's start with an overview. Everyone longs for a world made right, a world of beauty and joy, of togetherness, where things are right and good. It is no coincidence that this is a near-universal desire throughout time because it is what we have been made for. We've been made for a righteous and beautiful community, and while the desire for that reality is within us, we live in a world that is not right, far from beautiful, and fragmented. Just look around at the poverty, slavery, injustice, death, and depression surrounding you every day. Doesn't something in you suspect that there must be more than this?

A world free from injustice, full of purpose and bursting with beauty may seem like a fantasy, but I believe all of them will come true in the story of God one day. I would like to tell you about that story and help you find your place in it. You have a place in a grand story, a sweeping epic of love, joy, peace, and celebration. The story I'd like to invite you into is one of a world made right and beautiful, where everyone is brought together around God's resources and God Himself! It is no fantasy—it is a story of power, a transformational story that has been changing people for thousands of years. Before we consider this grand epic and your place in it, I want to tell you about my very first steps into the story of everything.

I'll never forget that ordinary day in late summer when light from another world came to my home. I was seven years old and we had just moved into our first real house. Before that, my family had been homeless off and on for the early years of my life. Living in and out of cars, abandoned homes, and random apartments seemed like an ordinary, normal way to live—as a child, I didn't know much better. That summer, however, my parents managed to get enough money together to rent what my brothers and I have come to refer to as the "farmhouse." It was nothing more than an old rundown house at the end of an old rundown street, but as I would learn, it was a place filled with wonder and magic.

The farmhouse had an old, musty, collapsing barn next to a field of mud. The muddy field was filled with remnants of a time gone by when the previous occupants grew corn and potatoes. Our life of poverty and displacement seemed as if it had come to an end with that little farmhouse. We moved in late into the summer and I'll never forget the first truly "ordinary" day of play. The day was hot and salty. My seven-year-old cheeks streamed with sweat and grit from a long day of playing in the field of mud and in that old barn. We had spent the entire day climbing trees, playing hide and seek, feeding bugs to spiders, and throwing mud and vegetables at each other. It was a dirty and hot day I'll remember forever! As the day ended and dusk fell, our mother called us inside. While we reluctantly lumbered toward the door, something magical began to happen. At the very end of that ordinary day, above that ordinary field, a sign of wonder began to appear just as night fell.

In the distance, I could hear ringing and clicking, a strange buzz that I've now come to know as a cicada bug. Stars began to fill the reddish-blue sky. It seemed as if the world had come to a holy hush for a moment of magic. Another world invaded that field, eclipsing the sweat and the grit and the mud. That invasion ushered us into a moment of wonder, awe, and joy that has marked me to this day. There it was, flickering over the field—blips of light, strange glows of green speckled above the mud and corn. In a trancelike state, my brothers and I stared into the night as that ordinary field flickered into an extraordinary stage of light and wonder. We grabbed an old Mason jar from the barn and ran into the field to capture light in a bottle. Within a few minutes we had a dozen or so phosphorous bugs glistening in our jars. We went yelling, "Mom! Our new house is magic! Look at these bugs with butts of light!" With a laugh, our mother began to explain what these extraordinary creatures were. As reasonable and scientifically sound as her explanation was, at the age of seven they were still magic to me.

In fact, now some forty-plus years later, whenever a field comes alive with little lights at dusk, my mind, my heart, my soul are connected to that moment when I was sure that the world was filled with magic. Fireflies to me are like an artifact from another world, something so wondrous I find it hard to believe they are just a normal, natural part of this world. Just maybe they are not. The fireflies stir that longing in us for magic, for a better world. Even more than that, they're a sign that the world I'm longing for—that we're all longing for—is real and interrupts and breaks into our world for brief moments full of light. The fireflies are harbingers of a world to come: a world that is invading ours, a world that is supposed to be and one day will be. When we get glimpses of such a world, I wonder, *What does my life today have to do with the bigger picture of it all?*

THE STORY OF EVERYTHING IS ALL AROUND US

The story of everything is unfolding all around us every day. Sometimes it's a whisper and sometimes it's a shout, but all around us are the smells, the sights and sounds, the texture of another world. In fireflies and

Beauty: *Manifest expressions of either naturally occurring or constructed elements of our experienced reality that elicit some emotional, physical, and/or mental pleasure.*

ocean waves, in the kindness of a stranger, in architectural design and fashion, and in the gut-shaking laughter of a family gathering—we see in our everyday lives proof of something more. That something more is another, better world invading ours. At first, we can only see it in little blips here and there. There is a story at play in our lives and in our world, the story of everything. This story focuses on a great invasion of another world that comes to us at first like blips of light hovering over the ordinary sweat and mud of everyday life. Your longings have been right all along. There is evidence of it all around us. Your dissatisfaction with *what should not be* points the way.

Beauty invades in bursts and moments but never stays for too long. Joy rises and sets, hope emerges and then retreats again like dusk and dawn. Back and forth like waking and sleeping, our world and the world to come sway and rock, calling and retreating, peaking and poking through the dusk. But when we learn the story of everything we begin to see that this other world is unfolding all around us, all the time. This other world can't be stopped; it is invading our lives and our world and it will one day come in full power. This world can be seen in moments of beauty and righteousness, in moments of wonder and awe. This world can be seen in simple things like the laughter of a child but also in complex things like differential equations and astrophysics. It just takes a Mason jar of faith and a willingness to run into the night. As scientific and as sound as the explanations may seem, a magic in the world is unfolding all around—a power in that world to come. And I, for one, believe that if we can embrace the wonder and run like a child again to the source of the light, *we will find our place in the story of everything.*

Now, when I keep talking about another world it isn't that our world is not valuable, or that our lives are somehow less important. In the story of everything we discover that the world to come makes sense of the world that is now. It brings meaning and focus to the lives we live, and it fulfills them. When the world to come collides with the world that is now, our world will be made right and beautiful; the world will be brought together like it is supposed to be. That's why there is a longing for light within us and all around us that confirms our deepest suspicions and our truest desires; that light says:

> *There actually is a purpose in this world, there is story to everything, and we have a place in it!*

That longing is trying to get us to understand the story of everything and pick up our Mason jars of faith and pursue something beautiful and right. That is what this book is all about.

YOUR GUIDE TO THE STORY OF EVERYTHING

Firefly Ideas are the things we must understand to grasp the story of everything, but they can be easy to miss or hard to understand because they are part of that other world. But when we encounter one of these Firefly Ideas in real life they stir that longing for something more. They break through in yellow-green blips and leave us believing that perhaps we and our world were made for something better and greater than we've ever known.

Throughout this book I'm going to be introducing you one by one to the Firefly Ideas I've observed, and explaining what they teach us about the story of everything. You'll see throughout the book these Firefly Ideas defined in the orange bars. Don't worry if you get a little muddled along the way; there's a glossary in the back that should help keep things straight. That ordinary field filled with an extraordinary beauty from an insect carrying light in its belly began to stir in me the desire to find my place in the story of everything. That moment of beauty and wonder set an irreversible course in my life.

The word *extraordinary* means beyond what is usual, ordinary, or established. Now, there is nothing wrong with normal things. We love all kinds of everyday things, but there is something crazy good, amazing, and joy filled about the extraordinary elements of life. These are the essential ingredients in the story of everything because they create a longing in us. C. S. Lewis writes, in the words of Psyche in his retold myth *Till We Have Faces*, "It was when I was happiest that I longed most." She says because the world was so beautiful, "it set me longing, always longing. Somewhere else there must be more of it."[1]

Beauty calls us in and shows us the way. The world around us points to the world to come either in the incongruence of its ugliness *or* in its beauty. It matters for everyone. Make no mistake about it: a story is unfolding, and we have a part to play in it.

This is where God comes in. The light from another world that can change everything is found in the story of God:

His story is the story of everything.

The story of God—the story of everything—will culminate in the fulfillment of our greatest hopes, desires, and longings around deep connection with others and with God Himself. The greatest expression of soul-fulfilling beauty is found in community with God Himself at the center. Scot McKnight explains, "With God at the center, we will be intoxicated with the deep, ecstatic joy of being known by God and knowing God. Plus, with God at the center, all pleasures will lead toward God, all happiness will be aimed at God, and all our pleasures will be attuned to God's pleasures."[2]

The story of everything is ultimately about the beauty and bounty we find with God and with one another in the context of a relationship with Him—but we are getting ahead of ourselves. What we can say at the start is that when we enter this story, we find what we've been looking for, and our faith in God becomes the source of doing beautiful things in the lives of others. This is how it all works. With God we can do what it is we've been longing to do. This is how the world to come collides with our lives and with the world around us.

LIGHT SHINES BEST IN DARKNESS

There is also a cost. We will talk about hard things like *sacrifice* and *risk*, about what it cost God to let us join in this story with Him. And about the cost it requires of us, about the sweat and dirt of life, which is necessary to experience the beauty of righteousness and togetherness. But for now, let's just begin with the warning, "light shines best in darkness."

In the United States, fireflies don't generally exist west of Kansas. The conditions are not conducive to sustain their colonies. Fireflies don't exist at all in many parts of the world. We in the Midwest and the East are blessed with an amazing bug with a lighted rear end—strange, isn't it? Trying to explain a field of light powered by beautiful insects to those who live in places where they don't occur is hard. We can show pictures or video loops of dancing light above the mud and corn, but it isn't the same as watching the night flicker green against lush trees and tall grass set to the music of cicadas. The glory of fireflies is revealed in certain places and under certain conditions, the chief of which is darkness.

As I said, light shines best in darkness, and in the same way the beauty, righteousness, and community of God shine best in places of despair and need, in the muddy fields of broken lives and forgotten dreams.

If you find a firefly in the daytime, you'll see that there isn't much extraordinary or beautiful about it at all. In fact, in the daylight you might mistake a firefly for any number of common beetles. It isn't until the darkness comes that you can see the glory of a firefly. This is how the story of God works too. We see the glory of God best in times of darkness, above the dirty, common, ugly conditions of the world. The people and places of our world are a lot like my farmhouse's dilapidated barn and leftover muddy field. I believe the broken and desperate people and places of the world can be transformed by a supernatural light. This light from another world is at the very center of the story of everything. By capturing this light, trusting God for ourselves, I believe we become a powerful, irreversible source in the world capable of doing beautiful and righteous things together. The people who discover their place in the story of everything get to become carriers of this very glory of a light from another world—a light that has the capacity to change the darkness of this world.

A few years ago, I traveled to Cambodia, doing work for an anti-trafficking campaign I was conducting.

Light shines best in darkness, and so the beauty, righteousness, and community of God shine best in places of despair and need, in the muddy fields of broken lives and forgotten dreams.

#dosomethingbeautiful

While on that trip, I met many impressive people, important government and military officials, NGO and university leaders, and business owners. But the most impressive, most extraordinary person I encountered in Cambodia was a man I had to meet in a secret building, in a secret room full of darkness. I'll call him D for short. I had heard of D for some time and wanted to speak with him. D was a legend in the anti-trafficking work going on in one of the dirtiest and darkest places on earth for the sex trafficking of the very young. D was the intelligence behind some of the most epic raids on brothels, freeing sex slaves as young as six and eight years old. I was brought into that dark room where D sat alone, wearing sunglasses. I had spent the earlier part of that day with some of the children D and his team had rescued from brothels and who were now ordinary children full of light and smiles, safely playing and going to school in a nearby compound for trafficking survivors.

None of these children had ever met D. They had no idea how this man sitting in a secret dark place had impacted their lives. They only knew that they were free, that light had come. Years before D had seen for himself the light of God and found his place in God's story. He was an ordinary person doing extraordinary things because at some point in his life he had an experience with God that caused him to seek out beauty and righteousness in the world around him. During my brief visit with D, I thanked him for his

hard work and he simply said, "It is an honor to
do what I am doing for God." The light D has in his
Mason jar of faith is extra-bright, however, because he
is doing something beautiful and right in a dark and
dirty place—where light shines best.

Our place in God's story of everything revolves
around first seeing the light ourselves, then embracing
it as our own, and finally carrying that light into
the world around us by sharing it with others and
by doing the righteous and beautiful things of God
together.

CHAPTER 1

A WORLD MADE RIGHT

The first major theme of the story of everything is that God intended for the world to be perfect—entirely and completely right. A world *nearly* right is not enough. God desires us and the world around us to be made *completely* right with Him. Our deepest suspicions and demands are that the world be made *right* right now! This is more proof that we are part of a big story, a story that encompasses everything around us. In our everyday longing for things to be right, we see how we were made for a perfect world.

Although some days in life are like a storybook and some are like a nightmare, our wedding day was as near to perfect as it could be. My wife and I were spending our wedding night at the finest hotel in town before flying out in the morning for our honeymoon. I remember the gold luggage carts spun atop granite floors; bellhops marching to the beat of ubiquitous, aromatic music; exuberant and earnest staff waiting on our every need. Our world on our wedding day was *nearly* perfect; all was *nearly* right—with one glaring exception. Just days before our wedding, I slipped during an ice storm and broke my ankle. I still remember the gasp of hundreds of wedding guests when I walked into the church sanctuary for the ceremony—not even my own mother knew I had broken my ankle. The accident happened during a crippling early spring storm. In the days before the wedding, all I could do was get bandaged and booted up while taking care of all the last-minute wedding plans, and so nobody knew about my accident. Showing up on our wedding night on crutches made the staff of the fine hotel even more energized to serve us. They rolled out the red carpet, adding all kinds of optional services to our stay at no extra cost. We were treated like a king and queen, and all was *nearly* right in our world, all except my broken ankle.

There is a significant difference between a very high-end hotel and the vast majority of what I now experience as a frequent traveler. As a conference speaker, I spend between 120 and 140 days away from home each year, and I've become painfully aware of the nuanced differences in hotel accommodations. Most of the time, a hotel experience is what I would call "adequate": a free snack, a warm breakfast, a nearly clean room, reliable Wi-Fi, and a "good enough" television. Every now and then, however, I am able to enjoy something special, like I did on my wedding night. While the brushes with hotel greatness are certainly few and far between, the difference is simply astounding. Fresh strawberry blintzes served by gloved and polished waitstaff, the clanking of real silverware against fine china plates, turndown service with plush robes, spa treatments where I am called by name. I can count on one hand the times I've had these experiences, and I certainly count myself among the lucky few who have. Most people will never visit this kind of hotel, and were it not for the generosity of others, I may have never done so either. Hobbling into that hotel on my wedding night made my day nearly perfect, but it was also the beginning of a realization, an awakening of sorts. You see, now I know what I've been missing and it has tainted me for good and for bad as a frequent traveler.

Whether or not you travel often, this disparity plays itself out in all kinds of places all around us every day. There is another level to almost everything—a hidden set of upgrades usually reserved for the wealthy and powerful. Whether one is experiencing baseball games, movie theaters, shopping, hotel stays, or air travel, there is almost always a secret and expensive version of most services and events. In some ways, it would be better to never have known very high-end treatment than to do so and not be able to experience it again. In some ways, my few brushes with hotel greatness have tainted my frequent "adequate" hotel stays. "Good enough" in the back of my mind is always defined by what I know could be: a better bed, better food, generous and attentive staff, and pampering. The great news is that hotel stays, good and bad, are not everyday reality. They are temporary experiences based on nothing more than a financial transaction. The entire visit is compressed into a hotel bill. However, something profound in the hotel stay gives us a glimpse into the story of everything.

BOUNTY IN A GOOD WORLD POINTS US TO THE BOUNTY OF THE WORLD TO COME

The one thing all very high-end hotel experiences have in common is that they hint at an aspect of the story of everything we'll call "bounty." Bounty in this world points us to a hint that there should be something more and that there will be something more in the world to come. The gold luggage carts, the hotel emblems embossing each granite entryway, the white gloves, and the ever-present and smiling staff of very high-end hotels express excess, luxury, and personal care. My definition of the word *bounty* is "A wide variety of good things given freely and in large amounts." The idea of bounty, then, has these four contours:

- variety,
- goodness,

- free or "unrecompensed," and
- abundance.

Fancy hotels are nearly perfect. They come very close to this concept of bounty with one exception, the cost, which makes them unavailable to most people. Nothing is free in the hotel transaction—not really. Even the smiles come at a fee in the end as they are tucked neatly into the cost of the overall service for the stay. The "given freely" aspect of bounty is nearly unheard of in our world. This, however, is where we see the very center of the story of everything unfold. In the ultimate conclusion to the story of God, there is wild, extravagant bounty offered freely to all people. Although we do a pretty good job at creating "near perfect" days for special occasions like a wedding, it comes at a price that very few can afford. In contrast, God is in the process of creating a world of variety, goodness, and abundance that, while costly (we'll get to that), is offered to all peoples free of charge.

Growing up poor and often homeless, my family was always on somebody's radar. People often want to do things for those in need. Some of the reasons people offer help are good and altruistic; others are bad and merely serve the person who is "helping." When you are the person always receiving help, determining which kind of "help" you are getting is pretty easy, even for a child.

One Christmas my mother drove my brothers and me to the store where she had registered us in a shopping spree with Santa for underprivileged kids. The store was closed, open only to the few children who had been accepted by the community group sponsoring the event. Our sponsor greeted us at the door, welcomed us in, and gave each of us a voucher worth thirty dollars! I felt like lucky Charlie in his chocolate factory with the winning golden ticket. The sponsor told me that I could buy *anything* in the store. *Anything!* I was overwhelmed by both the size of the store and the amount of money I had to spend. My sponsor chaperoned me up and down the aisles. For the first five minutes or so, he seemed as excited as I was, but quickly he became distracted, looking at his watch and asking me over and over again if I had made my choices. I took my time, however, choosing a gift for each of my brothers and my mother before determining how much I had left over to spend on myself. Of course, the gifts I was buying my family were all in the three- to six-dollar range to leave the bulk of the money for me—it only stands to reason.

After putting a few items in my cart, I told my sponsor I needed to go to the record section (this was the mid-1970s, so we're talking vinyl!). There I didn't need any time at all. I made my way to an all-black album on display with Gene Simmons covered with makeup along with the three other band members from my favorite rock band—Kiss! "I want Kiss Alive 2!"

The sponsor said, "That's inappropriate, kid. Why don't we go look at the toys?"

Immediately, I threw his words back at him. "You *said*! You said *anything* in the store! This is what I want!" Looking at his watch, the sponsor said, "Whatever. Knock yourself out." I picked the album up with excitement, holding it by its edges so as not to smudge the artwork, and made my way to the checkout counter with him.

At the end of the shopping spree, the local newspaper shot a photo with all the sponsors and their organization's sign. After the picture the sponsors took off and the kids scattered back to their parents. It was a glorious day of self-indulgence and self-congratulations. Both the person giving the gifts and the children receiving the gifts were mutually benefited, as documented by the local newspaper. Helping went both ways that morning. I felt I owed nothing to that man or his group; he seemed to benefit from the event as much as I did.

I spun that record over and over for years to come, and with each spin I remembered that day vividly, the day when I received a wide variety of good things given freely to all registered children by people trying to help. Giving and receiving in the *normal* world is often like this, but in God's story, it is not. As the recipient in the story of everything, we cannot give anything back to God. There is no "recompense," no possible repayment or mutual contribution we can give when God is involved. All of our "doing" for God is meaningless compared to what He did (and does!)

God invites us to good things, not the least of which is a relationship with Him—a covenant relationship, where we belong to God and to the people of God!

#dosomethingbeautiful

for us. And He gives not out of guilt for being wealthy, but freely and gladly to those who don't deserve it.

GOD'S DINNER TABLE IS SET!

God's gifts to us are not like a shopping spree where we selfishly indulge our wants (whether they're good for us or not). True bounty, the bounty God is offering, is more like a family feast where we are included not in a posed photo op but at the actual table. In Isaiah 55:1–3 we see God's invitation to bounty, an invitation that is both for today and ultimately for all peoples in the forever after of the story of God:

> "Come, all you who are thirsty,
>   come to the waters;
> and you who have no money,
>   come, buy and eat!
> Come, buy wine and milk
>   without money and without cost.
> Why spend money on what is not bread,
>   and your labor on what does not satisfy?
> Listen, listen to me, and eat what is good,
>   and you will delight in the richest of fare.
> Give ear and come to me;
>   listen, that you may live.
> I will make an everlasting covenant with you,
>   my faithful love promised to David."

Now, doesn't that sound like a dinner bell, a great invitation to a fantastic five-diamond hotel feast?!

This is a picture of God's story. This is a snapshot into God's heart, a heart that longs to sound the dinner bell and set the table where all are invited.

What this means for you personally is that God has invited *you*, specifically *you*, to His dinner table of bounty. God doesn't just love the world; He loves the specific people of the world. God's great story, called the kingdom of God, is unfolding throughout the world, but it never unfolds without a specific invitation to each and every one of His precious children. In this invitation, you should read God's invitation to you, not just to the world around you. For some people, it is easier to think of God's love for the world or for the people around them than it is to think about God's love for them personally. Reread the words of Isaiah, but where you see the word *you*, put your name in and see what it would be like for God's great invitation to the story of everything to be made out to you!

At God's table a wide variety of good gifts are given freely and in large amounts. Without "recompense" or repayment, God invites "everyone" to come to the table and enjoy these good gifts. And the most valuable gift we enjoy when we come to the table is a relationship with Him—a covenant relationship, where we belong to God and to the people of God! This is the very core, the center of the bounty God is offering.

Bounty is expressed in physical abundance, like a great feast at the table. It's seen in the connection and intimacy between the people around the table. But the most valuable and indispensable aspect of bounty is the relationship we have with the host of the feast, God Himself. Famous and somewhat controversial missiologist Stanley Hauerwas talked about a "story-formed community" as the primary way to understand our place in the story of God. He says, "A people are formed by a story which places their history in the texture of the world."[1] We become a people, a meaningful community, as we find ourselves together involved in a greater story than just the story of the individual.

His provision for His people goes beyond our physical needs and extends to things like love, belonging, relationship with Him, and togetherness with each other. We see this in every single aspect of the story of God. In the garden of Eden, God planted a well-positioned garden, made it aesthetically pleasant with trees that flourished and grew fruit to feed the newly established community, Adam and Eve. What made the garden a place of true bounty, however, was the fact that God was there, that He walked with Adam and Eve daily, that they were all together. The promised land God invited Moses to bring the Israelites into was a land so full of bounty that it was described as good, spacious, and flowing with milk and honey. What made the promised land so special, however, was that God chose to make His home there, to dwell with His people as a foreshadowing of a time when God would make His dwelling with us.

The story of God is punctuated with imagery of wedding feasts, singing and dancing, festivals, art and architecture, rich food and wine, but most of all, relationship with Him. The story of God is about making things right and people whole, binding up broken hearts and ankles. True bounty is God's ultimate intent because it is in His nature. God is a God of bounty! Most of the time in our world, bounty is seen as wasteful, luxurious, or excessive—because we almost always experience a cheap counterfeit of true bounty. We experience "near-bounty," broken expressions of bounty that cost us more than we have, are not intrinsically good, or lead to division between the haves and the have-nots of the world.

That's why when we chase after near-bounty it never satisfies us, because even if we can get into that fancy hotel, it is all a cheap imitation of what we've been designed for. Even if we found a way to get around problems of exclusion through expense, we still fail to experience true bounty because we forget true bounty is intertwined with a relationship with God. Bounty is bound up with being made right with God, and it requires a relationship with Him. All the active expressions of God, including creation, salvation, and restoration, are gifts of true bounty. The story of everything ultimately leads us to the experience of knowing Him personally, and that requires something beyond justice, something called "righteousness."

GOING BEYOND JUSTICE

The next Firefly Idea we'll look at is Righteousness.
Bounty is about the world made right. Righteousness
is about people being made right so they can participate in and contribute to Bounty. Humans long for
both Bounty and Righteousness, but neither can be
obtained unless God makes it happen. And both are
built on relationship with Him. The etymology of the
English word *righteousness* dates back to the early
sixteenth century, to an Old English word meaning
rightwise. The fullest sense of "rightwise" goes beyond
justice or justification; it goes beyond being in the
right or morally acceptable—it means to to participate
in and contribute to the bounty in the world.

Righteousness: *The state of being made morally
acceptable to God.*

*The experienced reality of righteousness, at least
from the English etymology, is bounty!* The theological
word in the Bible for righteousness, however, means
simply to be morally acceptable to God, to be right.
The great news is that the reality of a person who is
right with God (we'll talk shortly about how that can
happen) is bounty. We see this in Ephesians 1:3–14,
where the bounty of the righteous is described. In
this passage we see how God gives freely and in large

amount the wide variety of good things to those who have been made "rightwise" with Him:

> Praise be to the God and Father of our Lord Jesus Christ, who has blessed us in the heavenly realms with every spiritual blessing in Christ. For he chose us in him before the creation of the world to be holy and blameless in his sight. In love he predestined us for adoption to sonship through Jesus Christ, in accordance with his pleasure and will—to the praise of his glorious grace, which he has freely given us in the One he loves. In him we have redemption through his blood, the forgiveness of sins, in accordance with the riches of God's grace that he lavished on us. With all wisdom and understanding, he made known to us the mystery of his will according to his good pleasure, which he purposed in Christ, to be put into effect when the times reach their fulfillment—to bring unity to all things in heaven and on earth under Christ.
>
> In him we were also chosen, having been predestined according to the plan of him who works out everything in conformity with the purpose of his will, in order that we, who were the first to put our hope in Christ, might be for the praise of his glory. And you also were included in Christ when you heard the message of truth, the gospel of your salvation. When you believed, you were marked in him with a seal, the promised Holy Spirit, who is a deposit guaranteeing our inheritance until the redemption of those who are God's possession—to the praise of his glory.

Take a second and reread these verses slowly. Notice that, as we've seen before, the bounty of God includes things like belonging, blamelessness, joy, forgiveness, unrecompensed eternal riches, knowledge, wisdom, hope, inheritance, life, and connection to God and to God's children through the Holy Spirit. But notice too how all this Bounty is tied to being "rightwise." These gifts are jam-packed here at God's dinner table in just fourteen verses. This is just one of many passages in the Bible that tell us what the experienced reality is like for those made "rightwise."

Righteousness requires that a person or world be just, but it is much more than mere justice. You see, justice focuses on rights, on equity, on restitution; but righteousness is fundamentally about bounty. Justice makes someone pay what is owed; righteousness comes to us without "recompense" or required payment. God gives righteousness freely, liberally, to all who come and get it while it's hot! Justice *is* important, but it only balances the scales to equality, to what is due. Beyond justice, as a totally free and unearned gift, we see righteousness. Righteousness isn't about earning a cosmic merit badge or feeling like a better person than someone else; righteousness is about experiencing abundance, bounty, eternal life, which includes things like joy, belonging, hope, togetherness, and so much more.

God wants to give us many things, but He wants to start with righteousness. Righteousness is not merely the absence of wrong, but the presence of what is right, beautiful, and true—the experienced reality of bounty. For many people, our longing for a world made right—a world with God's true Bounty—begins with the desire for justice. But mere justice by itself is always dissatisfying, isn't it?

We can never experience a world "made right" simply by establishing justice. Justice is merely the doorway through which we must walk to get to righteousness. Even when justice wins the day, so much more is needed to have an experience of bounty. Imagine someone who is falsely incarcerated but set free after years of suffering. He may have finally gotten justice, but he is not living into the blessing of bounty. A community that suffers under the tyranny of a despot may be freed through winning a war or fleeing their land, but the ravages of death, displacement, disease, and despair along the way fall far short of bounty. The story of God does, in fact, include the establishment of justice, but the great news is that it goes much, much further.

THE STORY OF EVERYTHING IS LIKE A WEDDING

When Jesus began His public ministry, He chose to do so during the bounty at a wedding feast. While the wedding feast was happening, Jesus' mother begged Him to intervene in a small crisis. The wine had run out when the party was far from over. Jesus responded with the first "sign" of His power and identity. In John 2:6–11 we read,

Nearby stood six stone water jars, the kind used by the Jews for ceremonial washing, each holding from twenty to thirty gallons.

Jesus said to the servants, "Fill the jars with water"; so they filled them to the brim.

Then he told them, "Now draw some out and take it to the master of the banquet."

They did so, and the master of the banquet tasted the water that had been turned into wine. He did not realize where it had come from, though the servants who had drawn the water knew. Then he called the bridegroom aside and said, "Everyone brings out the choice wine first and then the cheaper wine after the guests have had too much to drink; but you have saved the best till now."

What Jesus did here in Cana of Galilee was the first of the signs through which he revealed his glory; and his disciples believed in him.

Signs are more than miracles. They are also prophetic metaphors pregnant with meaning. Signs are events that show us the world to come, what God is like, artifacts of another time and space. This particular sign is important because it is the first in the story of Jesus. This sign shows us the nature of the world we were made for, the world God is in the process of creating. In this sign we see the very core of the story of everything, and we see our place in that story! This sign places value on joy and celebration, togetherness and community. It acknowledges the centrality of bounty. This sign has nothing to do with what is adequate; in fact, just the opposite. It is about large amounts of very high-end wine. It is about breaking with tradition to lavish people with something truly extraordinary. This sign "revealed his glory" as well, meaning that it unveiled the essential nature of Jesus Christ and the story He seeks to establish.

Here it is, our "firefly idea." Bounty is the experienced reality of righteousness of those made right with one another and made right with God! In the next chapter, we'll consider doing something right, but first we need to ask the question, "How do I *become* right?" This is the fundamental question that will drive everything else. In the story of everything, we understand that something went wrong, much worse than a broken ankle in an ice storm.

Bounty: *A wide variety of good things given freely and in large amounts.*

Right in the beginning of human history, there was a major, earth-shattering, heartbreaking detour. Adam and Eve decided to turn their eyes to "near-bounty" by seeking a bounty that came without God. In fact, it came in opposition to Him and with that decision they became "un-rightwise." They came under His wrath, subjects of His justice. That decision became an infection that has been passed on to every single man, woman, and child personally and has also broken every culture of every people group, every structure and system throughout all time. The decision to seek near-bounty without a relationship with God brought just the opposite of bounty—it brought want and need, death and pain, despair and destruction. That decision was a "sign," an indication of humanity's true desire to live life, to enjoy life, to consume life without God at the center.

God had told them they would die if they ate the fruit. And even if all the ramifications of that one decision could never have been known at the time, through that one decision came a spiritual infection the Bible refers to as "sin." Sin is a hereditary spiritual darkness. Like it or not, you have it and so does every single person in the world. From the beggar on the streets of Bangalore to the richest man on earth, all of us have a darkness within that disqualifies us from the bounty of God. This spiritual infection shows up in the symptoms of life. We see it in things like greed, envy, lust, hatred, racism, abuse, self-indulgence, gossip, and other maladies. These maladies do not make us unrighteous; we are unrighteous to start! They are the symptoms of our unrighteousness. These symptoms do, however, require justice. Remember, justice is the doorway through which we *must walk* to have the experienced reality of bounty—a relationship with God. A relationship with anyone, let alone God

Himself, requires grace and mercy. God's grace is not "leniency," as if God is soft on unrighteousness. Mercy in a relationship with God is about His understanding of our limitations because of the condition we have. We are sickened with sin; we have a spiritual disease, and because of this, God is patient and slow to anger. God strives with us and it is in the striving that we experience a moment-to-moment "mercy" from God. Why does God give mercy? Simply because what He is ultimately after is a relationship of love and that just can't happen if justice and mercy are at odds with each other. God is both just and merciful, and He is able to be both because of Jesus. Jesus paid our debt, and without that payment there could be no merciful justice, no grace whatsoever.

THE FIRST STEP INTO THE STORY OF EVERYTHING

If we are going to be made right with God and enter into the story of everything, justice must be met first. The story of everything is not primarily about justice; however, it is the first step into the story of righteousness and what is ultimately beautiful. The justice that addresses the infection of sin and the consequences of our symptoms is itself the greatest expression of the bounty of God.

The entire bill for our sin was given to Jesus instead of to us. Even though He was "rightwise," having no sin, He paid the penalty for all that we've done and left undone when He died on the cross. His death on the cross pays the penalty for our wrongdoing, and the blood He shed has become the medicine to cure us from the infectious source of our maladies . . . sin itself. When we choose to acknowledge this great gift of recompense Jesus provides through His death, we can then receive the power to be made right with God. When we acknowledge that Jesus paid our debt, we can receive a "paid-in-full" receipt and experience the true bounty of a relationship with God.

Allowing Jesus to step in and pay our debt enables us to enter the story of God by *following Him* as our leader or master-teacher. While the turning of water into wine was Jesus' first sign, and it promised great Bounty to come, His greatest sign came in His death and resurrection from the dead, which made a way for anyone who would trust Jesus with their life to be free from their unrighteousness, become righteous, and partake in God's great bounty. Because Jesus rose from the dead, He is alive, we can follow Him today, and we can experience the righteousness that comes from a relationship with Him. Sounds like fireflies, doesn't it? It is God's cosmic dinner bell—seemingly too fantastical to be true, nevertheless it is. God says come, acknowledge your thirst, and eat and drink without payment; come to Me and experience intimacy through a covenant relationship with Me. As you are reading these words and you are sensing a desire to be made right with God, I want you to stop and consider saying these words out loud to God,

God, I want to be made right with You. I want to know You. I acknowledge that Jesus paid the debt for all that I've done and not done, and I receive the gift of His death in my place. I ask that You cure me from the infection of sin through the medicine of the blood of Jesus. Come into my life and lead me. I want You to be the Lord, the leader, of my life. Thank You for welcoming me into Your kingdom! I believe You are alive, Jesus. I believe You were raised from the dead, and I'm asking You to forgive me and include me at the dinner table You have prepared.

The words themselves can be said in different ways, but saying this to God is how we answer His invitation to come to the table, acknowledging that Jesus is the only way for us to both be made right and to experience the bounty of being right with God. This is the first step to finding our place in the story of everything and will ultimately lead us to a place where we can do beautiful things with God. This is the way we begin to live into bounty. Becoming right with God is the first step to doing something right, of becoming a source of bounty to the world around us. To be made right and to experience Jesus, we need to receive His righteousness. This not only changes our lives now; it prepares us to be a part of His forever family in the world to come. In my book *Making All Things New: God's Dream for Global Justice*, I wrote,

Our righteousness comes as a gift from God, and all righteous acts are only made possible only because of the grace and empowerment of God. We will be clothed—made acceptable—to participate in this day of days because the Lamb was slain, providing the righteousness necessary to gain entry into the wedding feast of all time. This is a prerequisite of being able to experience the dream of God. Without the righteousness of Christ—these clean and bright linens—we would never experience the joy of this day.[2]

Jesus is not a nice add-on to our lives—He is everything. We need Him if we are to have righteousness, experience righteousness, and eventually participate in a world of righteousness. Taking this step to acknowledge Him is the beginning of finding our place in the story of everything!

CHAPTER 2

DO SOMETHING RIGHT

The smell from the pumpkin-spice candle wafted through the open screen door. I was unloading my car after returning home from a long trip away from my family, having been out of the country for nearly two weeks. Fall was coming to an end. Vibrant red and yellow leaves littered my walkway and crunched under the weight of my luggage, announcing my arrival to my wife and kids. "Daddy's home!" they yelled as they burst through the door, grabbing hold of me with all their arms as if to pull themselves inside me. "That was too long, Daddy!" "I thought you'd never come back!" We cried a bit as each person took their turn to fully and lovingly embrace me. My luggage became an afterthought at the door as my favorite meal waited, warm and served up with love. I collapsed into my well-worn couch, cozy with blankets, pillows, and the people I loved most in the world.

Embrace. It is more than a welcome mat or even a firm handshake. To be embraced is to be enveloped, to feel the warmth of love, to know at the core of yourself that you are safe and accepted. To embrace the other is to offer these things to another person. Only in the context of relationships can we rightly experience the great firefly idea of embrace, which has the flavor and smell of things like grace, hope, and love.

Embrace is one of the most tangible ways people access grace, hope, and love. Admittedly, it is easy to embrace the people we love this way, particularly when the heart has grown fond through separation. The embrace required to do something right can be much more difficult. But it is essential that we learn to embrace the unembraceable since embrace is at the heart of righteousness and bounty. Embrace is how we experience bounty ourselves and how we share it with others. When we are embraced we get a taste of bounty. It allows us to feel, smell, taste, and touch bounty in a way we simply never could otherwise.

When we embrace others we, just for a moment, help make the world, and ourselves, right. So when we embrace others, especially when we embrace the unembraceable, we multiply bounty and righteousness in our world. In other words we do something right. This is essential in knowing God and finding our place in the story of everything. New York pastor Tim Keller says it this way in his book *Making Sense of God*: "Through faith in the cross we get a new foundation for an identity that both humbles us out of our egoism yet is so infallibly secure in love that we are enabled to embrace rather than exclude those who are different."[1] I encountered this truth the hard way on the streets of Detroit just after becoming a Christian.

During the rise of the AIDS pandemic in the 1980s, I lived in a small, dirty, and violent part of the Detroit area called Inkster. Toxic fumes, crack cocaine, and boarded-up homes greeted me each day as I made my way to and from college. I was not living in a place of bounty, and as an atheist I wasn't too interested in doing righteousness. I was looking out for myself, protecting myself, seeking my own self-interest at all times. In Detroit at the time we had a bumper sticker phrase, "I Ain't Friendly!" It was a mark of pride after being dubbed the murder capital of the country around that same time.

I lived in a harsh world and I had a harsh view of the world. I was violent and self-absorbed to the point that I couldn't care less that people were dying all around me from gunshot wounds, drug overdoses, and AIDS. Back then, it was a common assumption that if you had AIDS, you were almost certainly a homosexual. As an angry, self-absorbed atheist, my thought and the thought of most around me was, *They are getting what they deserve. Why should anyone help them? They brought this on themselves.* Homophobia wasn't even a word in my world in the mid-1980s, but it sure was the experienced reality of it. Caring for those whom I thought were sick in mind and body was never even a consideration.

I became a Christian in 1989 just as the world's thoughts about AIDS and homosexuality were beginning to shift as well. At the same time I became a Christian, Detroit suffered an explosion of homelessness, particularly homeless men who were abruptly cut off from important social programs due to a change in political leadership. Several people from my church routinely went to the places where these men were flocking for care: to the warming centers, soup kitchens, and rescue missions of Detroit. I began developing a heart of compassion for the poor, thinking that I was following in the footsteps of Jesus. Little did I know how poor I was.

BEING EMBRACED BY THE UNEMBRACEABLE

One Sunday afternoon my friends and I went to a particularly hard-hit part of Detroit—Greektown. Homeless men sat and lay all over the street, vying for the pocket change of those who had come out to eat and play in the city's center. While working among these men that afternoon, I was challenged to the core when I met Frank. Frank was a newly homeless man who had spent his first week sleeping on the cold streets of Detroit. He had yet to develop the leathery skin and layered, tattered look of most of the other men; he seemed nearly normal. It was clear that the massive influx of homeless men was becoming a full-blown crisis. Most people were already getting tired of the Franks on the street, barring them from places of business and harassing them for their laziness.

Even though Frank appeared nearly normal, almost passing as "one of us," during my initial encounter with Frank I saw people hurl nasty insults at him as we tried to converse. "Frank," I asked, "would it be all right if we went to lunch and talked? I'd like to hear your story." Surprised but desperate, Frank agreed. We went down a few doors to a diner. As we entered, the manager immediately said Frank was not welcome, even though I was buying lunch. We ordered takeout and sat on the stoop outside the diner. As I sat listening to Frank's life story and how he had become homeless, I was caught by surprise when he included the fact that he had contracted HIV from his boyfriend, who had also just abandoned him. My inner world churned, a sweaty restlessness sank into my heart, and I began eyeing the street for my exit strategy. Just then, Frank burst into tears and said, "Why are you doing this for me? Nobody has stopped to look me in the eye all day; it is like I'm a leper. I don't know what to do and I don't know what I've done to deserve this, but thank you for looking me in the eye today—no one has done that all week!"

Frank was in a place of desperation. He was not experiencing the bounty of grace, hope, or love. To be honest, I had not embraced Frank that day; in fact, I don't even remember shaking his hand. Little did Frank know that inwardly I, too, despised him. I despised Frank for his homosexuality, for his disease. He did not know that I had very little grace or love for him, but for some reason Frank felt embraced by me simply because I saw him, I looked him in the eye.

Frank's ugly weeping, however, broke my heart. I yelled at myself inwardly, "York, you hypocrite! How can you say you love people when you are unwilling to meet them where they are at?" The only thing I could think to do in that moment was to embrace Frank. I half-reached out to him as he grabbed onto me in a childlike way. Weeping, Frank kept uttering the words, "Thank you, thank you, thank you." I remember the stinky steam rising from the nearby manhole cover, the glares from those eating on the other side of the glass window. I remember the pang of shame in my heart for my harsh thoughts and unloving posture toward the sick in body and "unembraceable" man now in my arms. It's easy to embrace and be embraced amidst the wide variety of good things we have in our lives—loving children, a favorite meal, a warm and safe home. It is hard to embrace the unembraceable amidst the sorrow of complicated circumstances, social ostracization, and the secret fear and hate in our hearts. But when we are made right as people it helps us find a way to do something right in the midst of the world's complexity.

BEING TRANSFORMED BY EMBRACE

Every one of us has our "Frank," a person who typifies the unembraceable. For some, it is their education and wealth; for others it is their poverty and lack of education. For some, it is a particular accent or skin color; for others it is their sexual orientation, religion, occupation, or family heritage.

Many things make people unembraceable to us. As followers of Jesus, we cannot grow in showing righteousness to others unless we grow in our capacity to embrace specifically those who seem unembraceable to us. This is where we start, where it is hard, not easy, amid stinky steam, desperate hugs, and glaring eyes. Doing something right is not always the same thing as doing something just. We can often do justice without embracing anyone at all, but we cannot give grace, hope, and love without embrace— that is impossible. Justice had little to do with Frank's needs in the moment. Frank needed something beyond justice; he needed grace, hope, and love experienced through embrace. Remember, justice is merely the doorway through which we must walk to make access to bounty possible.

Doing something righteous goes beyond justice— intentionally transcending the basic requirements of things like equity, punishment, and redistribution. There is a magic in righteousness that is not expressed in justice, an element of wonder that expands the soul and brings healing and hope to the world. Now, righteousness is never *at odds* with justice, but it transcends it, subsuming its basic and inadequate requirements. We unleash God's righteousness in the world when we embrace the unembraceable and allow grace, hope, and love to take root in our lives. Without the work of Jesus, we get stuck on trying really hard. But because of the bounty of Jesus' work in our lives, we *can* do something right through Him! Doing something righteous is one of the primary ways we live into the story of God, how we find our place in the story of everything. Your place in the story of everything is to be a person of embrace, not merely for the sake of those you embrace, but so that you can become more like Jesus, who embraced us. You live the best version of your life, finding your place in the story of everything, by allowing God's hard work of embrace through Jesus to change you from the inside out.

DOING RIGHTEOUSNESS IN AN UNJUST WORLD

Doing righteousness often creates an opportunity for something unusual and beautiful to happen. Most people in most places of the world most of the time are not experiencing anything near righteousness. If they are lucky, people live in a just community where things are relatively fair and even. Even this, how-ever, rarely exists. We create artificial communities of fairness in places like sporting arenas, university classrooms, and toll-based freeway systems. In these contexts, people play by the same rules, have equal

access to learning, and pay equal amounts to share
the same road. Like high-end hotels, however, these
spaces are artificial, and we eventually realize that
even in these places created to be fair, things like
wealth, race, family background, and other factors
create inequities from the beginning that then may
grow into injustices. Injustices are almost always
about bounty. Earlier in Isaiah's prophecy, we read
of how God is uniquely angered at the injustices the
"bounty-less" of the world face from their oppressors,

> Woe to those who make unjust laws,
>> to those who issue oppressive decrees,
> to deprive the poor of their rights
>> and withhold justice from the oppressed of my people,
> making widows their prey
>> and robbing the fatherless.
> What will you do on the day of reckoning,
>> when disaster comes from afar?
> To whom will you run for help?
>> Where will you leave your riches?
> Nothing will remain but to cringe among the captives
>> or fall among the slain.
>
> Yet for all this, his anger is not turned away,
>> his hand is still upraised. (Isa. 10:1–4)

The needy and poor, widows and orphans . . . these
are expressions of the "bounty-less." When they are
prevented from experiencing the bounty of God, God
is angered. Wherever there is lack or want around

resources, injustices flourish. Our world is broken by sin—inside and outside. We are all seeking bounty, but the bounty of this world often comes at the expense of someone else. That's why one of the first requirements of doing something right is working to ensure that all people have access to bounty.

Unfortunately, for the vast majority of people in our world today, this kind of justice is a luxury—things are not fair, wrongs are never righted, and bounty seems like something reserved for storybooks or movies. How can we live righteously in a world where even justice seems out of reach? While we do not live in a fair and just world, we can help others get to God's table of bounty. For thousands of years in the church, women and men have learned the secret of experiencing bounty while they and others around them are living in places of inequity. This is the secret of the story of everything, that we can have something more in a world continually plagued by inequities and injustices. We have bounty that can't be stolen and that is bought without money. Your place in the story of everything can be found in doing righteousness, particularly in a world of injustice—this is how you create beauty in the lives of those who've yet to come to God's family dinner table. You can point them to Him.

The good news is that we can have and experience bounty even when the world isn't fair. We can help others experience this same bounty along with us. This is where God's righteousness lights up the night sky because it defies the injustices and inequities of our world and the very circumstances of our lives. Experiencing bounty is first and foremost about knowing God and then choosing to join Him in what He is doing. When we know God and do the actions that God would have us do, we find that regardless of the circumstances, we experience something greater than justice, something more than mere riches—we experience the kingdom of God, the presence and power of God Himself! So then how do we know God and do the things God commands? We are first made right through Jesus, and from that place of relationship, we do righteousness.

HOW DO I KNOW WHICH "RIGHT" TO DO?

Now, the most significant way we begin to comprehend how to do righteousness is from the Bible, the primary way we know God and know the story of God. Without the Bible, we can never truly find our place in the story of everything. Take Isaiah 10 above for example. In many parts of the world, the poor have no rights; rights are reserved for the rich. The Bible teaches us, however, that the poor have rights too, so in order to have a world made right, it must include addressing not just the *needs* of the poor but also the *rights* of the poor. Regardless of what those rights may be, it is a *biblical* idea that the poor have rights. We cannot have an understanding of God's story or find our place in it without the recorded story of the Bible!

I was made right with God when I became a follower of Jesus—because of what He did, not because of anything I could do. As a result, I began to care about others, like Frank, a gay, homeless man on the streets of Detroit, in ways I had never done before. I began to do right too—growing in the expressions of the love God had put in my heart through His Spirit. I became able to embrace people who, before, were unembraceable to me. I became capable of doing righteousness because I had been made right with God. Doing righteousness is what we do when we've been made right with God. It is one of the ways we can tell if we have a relationship with Him. In the story of everything, then, we do the things that God requires of us because we have been made right.

One of my heroes is Noel Castellanos, the CEO of the Christian Community Development Association. In his book *Where the Cross Meets the Street,* Noel challenges us to see places of urban poverty as complex ecosystems of problems—requiring holistic, comprehensive, interconnected efforts. He paints a vision that brings together justice, proclamation, community restoration and development, and works of compassion as a sign of the kingdom's power and presence.[2] Noel's model for community transformation has had a lasting impact on the lives of countless people and has become a model for other organizations and civic entities in engaging their communities. What Noel and his tribe have come to understand about doing righteousness is that it is a complex, supernatural work that requires more than talk. It requires action.

The Bible tells us that doing righteousness can take many forms—caring for the poor is one way to follow Jesus' call on our lives. What the poor in our world need more than a one-off meal and a hug from a stranger are comprehensive forms of embrace that lead to true life transformation. Doing something right, then, is complex but worth it, as Noel and others have come to demonstrate. Doing righteousness among the world's poor, marginalized, oppressed, sick, and neglected has a great capacity to show God's story unfolding in our lives and in our world.

Doing something right and introducing God's truth into the darkness is always right, but doing righteousness where things are "wronger" is of critical importance. That's why I believe doing righteousness particularly where bounty is rare is what we should be doing whenever possible. No matter where you live, what your gifts are, and what resources you have . . . God's work where bounty (spiritual, emotional, financial, etc.) is rare is needed. And He invites us to be a part of it!

JESUS' ROLE IN THE STORY OF EVERYTHING

Providing bounty to people who have none is how we provide an awe-inspiring wonder. Perhaps that's why Jesus placed so much emphasis on the down-and-out, the marginalized, the sick, the demon possessed, and the shamed. At the beginning of Jesus' ministry, He chose an ancient quote from the book of Isaiah to announce His own role in the story of everything:

> He went to Nazareth, where he had been brought up, and on the Sabbath day he went into the synagogue, as was his custom. He stood up to read, and the scroll of the prophet Isaiah was handed to him. Unrolling it, he found the place where it is written: "The Spirit of the Lord is on me, because he has anointed me to proclaim good news to the poor. He has sent me to proclaim freedom for the prisoners and recovery of sight for the blind, to set the oppressed free, to proclaim the year of the Lord's favor."
>
> Then he rolled up the scroll, gave it back to the attendant and sat down. The eyes of everyone in the synagogue were fastened on him. He began by saying to them, "Today this scripture is fulfilled in your hearing."
>
> All spoke well of him and were amazed at the gracious words that came from his lips. (Luke 4:16–22a)

Jesus found that particular place in this long, dense, ancient book and chose it as self-declarative, saying that it had been fulfilled in the hearing of the people *that day*. Jesus chose these words to declare what His own role was in the story of everything. The presence and power of God Himself was made manifest through Jesus' self-declaration. What happens immediately after this in the story of Jesus is that He goes on to proclaim good news to the poor; He heals the blind and delivers those imprisoned by demonic spirits. Jesus goes on to freely provide a wide variety of good things in large amounts to many peoples—His power at work in the lives of those who suffer establishes the bounty of righteousness. He did all these things to display His power and to ultimately point to Himself as the one capable of freeing people from the captivity of sin!

In the reading of this ancient book, Jesus also says He was anointed to proclaim something called "the Lord's favor," an interesting phrase that showed Him to be the fulfillment of a special year celebrated only every fifty years by the Jews, the Year of Jubilee. In the Year of Jubilee debts were cancelled, slaves went free, things were made fair and equitable. Like Noel Castellanos's model of community transformation, the Year of Jubilee had to do with redistribution, reconciliation, empowerment, and the proclamation of good news. The Year of Jubilee was always especially good news to the poor and the slave and in places where things were not fair or equitable. It wasn't always such good news, however, for the people who were rich and powerful.

However, "the Lord's favor" goes beyond this Jewish marker Year of Jubilee—it was more than just physical good news. He came to forgive our sin debt. The phrase also speaks of God's determination to embrace the unembraceable. The word for "favor" in Jesus' mother tongue meant "accepted," and in this context it is being applied to the unacceptable: sick people, poor people, underprivileged people . . . Jesus shared this to show how the story of God is something beyond justice; it is a righteous story of bounty for

Embrace: *The act of holding something or someone in a way that demonstrates love, compassion, acceptance, and the value of that which is being held.*

all peoples that demonstrates grace, hope, and love through *embrace*. Jesus' role, then, in the story of everything is to embrace people, yes, and also to show them the way to Himself. This certainly does not mean that all God does is embrace—there is a cost to embrace. In fact, there is a terrible cost and that is the full wrath of God as judge. God is not just loving, He is holy. He cannot tolerate unrighteousness and will one day obliterate all evil. In God's mercy and love, He has poured out His wrath upon Jesus on the cross. One day Jesus will pour out that wrath back upon the world as well. We live in between these two great events—the day Jesus took wrath upon Himself on the cross and the day He will pour it back out upon the world in judgment. In this "in-between" time, then, the cost for the embrace of forgiveness has already been paid by Jesus. What is required of us is to reach out like a child, like Frank did to me, and receive it.

When we reach out to God, He doesn't half-hug us like I did with Frank. God willingly and fully embraces us but we must never ignore the cost that He paid in order to make that embrace possible.

In sum, Jesus Christ made possible the very idea of this one wonderful, earth-shattering concept— *embrace*. Through Him we are embraced by God and empowered to embrace others around us. This is what Jubilee is ultimately about. This was not such good news in His synagogue at the time, for while those in attendance were momentarily amazed at His words, immediately after Jesus spoke to them He was escorted out of town by force. The people of Jesus' own hometown tried to kill Him by throwing Him off a cliff because Jesus explained that the embrace of God was intended for all peoples, not just the Jewish people. The story of Jesus is a story of a God determined to embrace us, seek and save the lost, and offer His life as a ransom for many.

WE ARE TRANSFORMED AS WE PRACTICE EMBRACE

Once we accept God's embrace of us and recognize His rightful place in our lives, we start to see His grace, hope, and love expressed in and through us. We embrace because we are embraced by God. As we embrace the unembraceable, we find ourselves transformed. Embrace is hardest where we have the greatest potential for self-transformation. Where embrace is hardest is also where we have the greatest capacity to do something right. Throughout Jesus' ministry, it was the rich, the powerful, the ethnic insider, the religiously educated who most often got a good dose of Jesus' commitment to justice. Treasures of bounty such as grace, healing, and love through embrace were most often reserved in the preaching of Jesus to those living without such things. When Jesus did signs and wonders, healings and exorcisms, He almost always did so in contexts where people were hurting, where justice was rare, and where bondage and sorrow had become the acceptable norm. These are all expressions of the embrace of Jesus.

The real wonder on the streets of Detroit that day wasn't Frank's marvel that I had looked him in the eye, bought him a sandwich, or embraced him. Those are all nice things that are possible without God's intervention. The real wonder was that *my* heart broke for the things that break God's heart. *I* was transformed in that moment of embrace as I saw my lifetime of hatred and fear dissolve through Frank's gift of embrace to me. Without knowing it, Frank had been used by God to help me grow.

Our Mason jars of faith are filled through embrace, filled with a light that not only shines in the world around us but also lights up our lives as well. This is the magic of the story of everything. In all things, God is working not just to change some world out there, down the street, across the oceans, but the world inside of us. Magic. This is where transformation happens.

People who do not know Jesus are quite capable

of doing right things, often without knowing it. Frank and many others I've encountered have lives that are outside God's desire for them, yet God uses them to accomplish His desires in the world. We do not need to be Christians to *do* right things, but we do need Jesus for our right things to have lasting, eternal value and impact beyond a hug in the streets and a sandwich on a stoop. Women and men are capable of doing extraordinary things, magical things, because we are God's daughters and sons. We are simultaneously lost and marred by a soul-crushing disease we know as sin, but we are also transcendent, chosen vessels carrying the very face of the God of everything! We are full of wonder and determination, capable of beauty and love and the impossible! Even in our broken and marred state, we cannot rub the image of God off our souls even though we try with all the illicit sex and binge drinking and overspending and evil we can muster. We can *do* right things because we carry about within us the residual image of a righteous God, but because of sin, everything is stained.

Sin is like a dye pack in a bag full of cash that has exploded in our lives. It has stained us, our most valuable gifts and abilities, our surroundings, and anything we might have done with our freedom and dreams. Because of sin, our righteousness is not righteousness in the ultimate sense. Isaiah 64:6 reminds us, "All of us have become like one who is unclean, and all our righteous acts are like filthy rags;

we all shrivel up like a leaf, and like the wind our sins sweep us away." We need Jesus for our right things to be something more—something that actually, ultimately, contributes to the story of everything!

Doing something right is always the right thing to do, but (in addition to loving and serving those close to you) consider doing something right in the places and with the people that are furthest from bounty and furthest from your comfort zone as well. Micah 6:8 puts it this way: "He has shown you, O mortal, what is good. And what does the LORD require of you? To act justly and to love mercy and to walk humbly with your God." *Good* here is actually the Hebrew word for *bounty*. What this ancient, famous phrase means then is that bounty comes from God through the work of embrace. It is also important to note that the word for *love* means to be intimately aware

Mercy: *To give or receive that which is not deserved; to express or receive condescension without the expectation of recompense and not on the basis of merit.*

of or to have had deep experience with. We experience bounty and we establish bounty in the lives of others when we are intimately familiar with *mercy—* embracing the unembraceable.

Here it is, another firefly idea: grace, hope, and love are expressed *and* experienced through the mercy of embrace. This is how bounty "lives" in us and through us. Your place in the story of everything is to both experience bounty and be a conduit of that bounty to others through the work of embrace. We need to embrace the other both in complex, enduring ways and simple, literal ways. Bounty is established in our lives and the lives of others as we become experts in the mercy of embrace.

In God's embrace we are transformed, and we can then be a part of His transforming work of others by lifting the shame and reproach that comes from being unembraceable. Embrace transcends justice; it transforms us and our world because it is otherworldly, an artifact from a time and place of beauty and wonder. When we accept the embrace of God and are made right by Him, we begin to see our place in the story of everything. We become messengers of mercy in our world sent to embrace the unembraceable. Embrace is perhaps one of the highest forms of beauty we as humans can witness and experience. This is by design. God has designed us to be participants, not just observers, of this beauty. It is how the story of everything moves forward and expands.

Next, I want to challenge you to consider what it might look like to "walk humbly with your God" by doing something righteous. Instead of giving a list of examples, I want to challenge you to dream for yourself through the following questions.

DO SOMETHING RIGHT:

1. Who are the unembraceable people in my context?

2. What are the injustices or limitations they face?

3. What would it look like for them if these wrongs could be made right?

4. What could bounty look like in their lives?

5. What one practical thing can I do to embrace them personally?

6. What one practical thing can I do to introduce them to God's story today?

7. How could doing something right help me know God more about who God is?

CHAPTER 3

A WORLD MADE BEAUTIFUL

It was only mid-June but already the grass crunched under my feet like potato chips. We were just at the beginning of the great drought of 1988–89 in the US, one of America's worst. The ugliness of the earth was matched by the ugliness of my dead-end, drug-infested street. We were also at the height of the crack-cocaine epidemic in Detroit, and my community was as scorched by violence and drugs as the extra crunchy grass and trees in my front yard. My world was far from beautiful.

The burned-out houses on our block were constantly accessorized by drug addicts and drunks. The stink of toxic fumes from the nearby waste disposal plant hung in the dense, hot air along with the rattling speakers of rap music blaring from cars passing by. Beauty was far from my mind. People living in places like mine are far more concerned about things like food, safety, and shelter. Death was a way of life.

I had just graduated high school and my graduating class was missing several who were a part of the twenty-one homicides in my immediate neighborhood. Death from gunshot, death from drugs, death from disease, and death from suicide—beauty was nowhere to be found. That is why I was caught off guard by my mother's request. "York," she hollered authoritatively, "you are going to have to take care of the hedges in the front yard this summer." We had lived in the house for three years, and I had never even taken notice of the bushes in the front yard. My mother was recovering from surgery, so I was tasked with caring for the bushes. This small task in a place of death and ugliness, however, was one of the first ways I began to suspect that there was something more, a story about everything.

Surprisingly, caring for these bushes also launched a lifelong love for natural beauty, which I've cultivated into a talent for landscaping and gardening. This has become a core part of who I am today, but at the time I don't think I had ever stopped to take note of a tree, a bush, or a flower in all my life.

A row of seven bushes about five feet tall separated our house from the invading urban squalor. For some reason, this hedge did more than separate our house from the neighbors; it seemed to actually *do* something.

It kept ugliness from creeping over onto our property.
When I began to take care of the bushes, I wouldn't
have called them beautiful. They too were crispy
from the drought and filled with weeds. I began
by weeding, trimming, and excessively watering.
I then covered the ground around them with stones,
which I later learned would help with erosion and
water retention. I began to take small joy in seeing
new shoots and leaves, watching the bushes become
vibrant under my care. My teen friends laughed at
me as I spent hours each week nurturing bushes
for my mom. It didn't take long before this raggedy
row became lush and green and strikingly full of life
against a backdrop of ugly sounds, sights, and smells.
My friends laughed a little less over the summer as
they saw how my care made a small difference in
making something green in one of the worst droughts
in American history.

Though our house was ugly and the surrounding
area was terribly ugly, this simple, beautiful row of
vibrant bushes stood as a barrier, a marker against the
drug addicts, drug pushers, trash dumpers, homeless,
sleepy drunks, and others. Our house had a modicum
of respect because there was something living there,
something green, something beautiful.

WHAT BEAUTY IS AND WHAT BEAUTY DOES

Beauty is an elusive term, one often thought to be
merely subjective. Standards of beauty have changed

from era to era, from peoples to peoples. An element of personal taste goes into labeling something beautiful, but there is also a fixed element. An oversimplified, standard definition of beauty is: the right proportion and alignment of attributes in something or someone that brings deep emotional and/or mental pleasure to the beholder. Sounds pretty sterile, doesn't it?

When we are in the presence of beauty, our experience of it is far from sterile; it is transcendent. Google the term and you will get some combination of the elements of this sterile definition. But something is missing in this basic definition. Beauty is much more than a proper alignment of attributes. It goes beyond providing mere mental and emotional pleasure. Beauty actually *does* something. Beauty is functional. Because of this, beauty is the font that God uses to write the story of everything. God's beauty actually accomplishes something, as I learned during a time of ugliness and drought with those green bushes. The beauty of the bushes didn't just look good; their beauty offered a tangible protection against the ugliness surrounding us.

Part of the reason a concrete definition of beauty is hard to articulate is that beauty is one of those firefly ideas—it belongs to another realm. You know that you are in the presence of beauty, even in a basic simple expression like my bushes, by what beauty accomplishes both in us and in the world around us. Beauty can captivate us at a soul level. Beauty ushers in a "holy hush" most commonly experienced as eerie silence. Beauty is most striking when it stands against the backdrop of the ordinary and ugly. My simple row of bushes would never have stood out as beautiful if it weren't for the drought-ravaged lawn on which it stood. A normal, ordinary day became a magical wonder of beauty at dusk in that field of fireflies in part because of the ugliness of the home, dilapidated barn, and field of mud and corn.

We see this all the time. A sudden change in weather patterns can create an elemental display of natural beauty in a snowstorm, fog rolling across a still lake, or a thunderstorm flashing with bright light. Watch a person stare into a sunset, lose themselves as snow swirls about them, or forget the world around them as they gaze into a fireplace. Beauty beckons us into a half-conscious state where we are joyfully unconcerned with concern.

Think about when you have experienced something beautiful. How did it make you feel? Think about when you created something beautiful, perhaps a piece of art or a row of flowers or a table full of food. Whether we are experiencing or creating beauty, it beckons us. It calls to us. Open Instagram and scroll through the newsfeed of your friends. Do you find yourself a little lost on the more artistic shots, the shots of snow on mountain peaks, the shots of the beautiful smiles of your friends' children? Part of what makes our consumption of social media so addictive is not just the people in our feed but how they are often immersed in a vibrant world and radiating life. Social media for most people is not just about friendship; it is about the beauty of the world and the beauty of people. My phone has become for me a window into other worlds, often as powerful and inescapable as a fire in the fireplace or watching the sun dip low into Lake Michigan.

Regardless of whether we find beauty in the palm of our hand or in the natural world around us, we are subject to its power because of where beauty comes from. Beauty is a sneak peek through a portal into another time and place. It's an artifact of another world. Certainly, fireflies dancing against the backdrop of a summer meadow at dusk is a beautiful sight, but watch the people *watching* it and you'll see the power of beauty. Beauty enraptures us, holds us spellbound, and causes a reverent hush. But beauty does more than this. Beauty elicits within us a set of transcendent reactions. The word *transcendent* means that which is beyond our physical, visible experience. Transcendent reactions to beauty include hope, joy, longing, passion, and love. Beauty expands the interior of our hearts and minds and allows us to experience transcendence. Beauty actually accomplishes something. It opens a door within our souls to experience God's story of everything.

THE BEAUTY EFFECT

Because beauty does these things, I refer to the impact of beauty as "the beauty effect." The beauty effect changes us and the world around us. The beauty effect is how the story of everything gets told and even the point of the story itself. The most beautiful thing we can ever do with our lives is worship God. As we'll learn later, beauty is the whole point of the story of everything as it culminates in knowing God, glorifying Him, and enjoying Him forever. That is true and ultimate beauty, to know God and worship Him. On a smaller scale, however, when we are exposed to beauty, for even a moment or in some small way, the world is momentarily made right. My green, lush, and well-proportioned bushes opened something within me. I became alive to new possibilities that flew in the face of the ugly, smelly, dangerous world I assumed was normal. Through the contrast of green life against death, the beauty effect caused me to see that my world was not good or normal. The beauty effect created hope within me too, because in that ugly and dangerous place, I saw that I could change one thing; perhaps I could change others too. This is what beauty does!

Beauty is a great gift, coming out of God's love for us and His passion for the world. Makoto Fujimura, in his book *Culture Care*, says this:

> A Christian understanding of beauty begins with the recognition that God does not *need* us, or the creation. Beauty

is a gratuitous gift of the creator God; it finds its source and its purpose in God's character. God, out of his gratuitous love, created a world he did not need because he is an artist.

Beauty itself is not, in this sense, necessary. . . .

But even if we would agree that beauty is not necessary to our daily survival, it is still necessary for our flourishing.[1]

Fujimura demonstrates through this wonderful book that beauty is a gift that causes us and our world to flourish, and it is a part of the very understanding of flourishing. The beauty effect changes the *behavior* of people too. While I can't guarantee it was the green bushes that caused a change in others on my street, I do know that after these bushes were brought back to life, the normal violations of our space declined significantly.

Prior to the resurrection of these simple bushes, it was common to open the front door of our home and find a random man drinking liquor out of a brown paper bag or to find a used condom on our driveway. We wouldn't have thought twice about food wrappers and cigarette butts on our lawn or in our bushes. After these green bushes began to shine, these "normal" things became the exception instead of the rule. Beauty, even in its simplest forms, protects us from the worst versions of the world, ourselves, and the despair of hopelessness. That's because the beauty effect is not a side benefit, but a core part of flourishing, of living into the story of everything.

But beauty also demands something from us.
It calls us to rise. It creates a call to action and raises
concerns within us about what is good or normal.
It requires us to recognize the incongruence within
us and around us. Beauty is essential for being fully
human. The human longing for transcendence drives
us to beauty. Staring into the ocean, a fire, a swirling
snowstorm, a sunset; that trancelike state we see
in ourselves and others happens because in that
moment of consumption we are connected to the story
of everything. Our deepest longings are affirmed, our
secret suspicions about what *should* be are confirmed in
that moment when we are connected to transcendence
through the beauty effect. Like a moth drawn to a
flame, we have a hard time looking away. Consider the
call beauty has on our lives from God's creation:

> The heavens declare the glory of God;
>> the skies proclaim the work of his hands.
> Day after day they pour forth speech;
>> night after night they reveal knowledge.
> They have no speech, they use no words;
>> no sound is heard from them.
> Yet their voice goes out into all the earth,
>> their words to the ends of the world.
> In the heavens God has pitched a tent for the sun.
>> (Ps. 19:1–4)

God's creation is written in the font of beauty and we,
as a part of that creation, are connected at a soul-level

to it. We are not human without beauty, because in beauty we are most connected to ourselves, to others, and even to God Himself! The proof of this can be seen ultimately in worship. The ultimate expression of our humanity is expressed in worship, and in worship we are connected to God.

THE MEANS AND END OF BEAUTY IS WORSHIP

Toward the end of this world's story, the beauty of God Himself is revealed to all people. Unedited, unfiltered, unveiled, in the end God will be seen for all that He is. Although we can never experience the full beauty of God in this world without dying from exposure, in the world to come followers of Jesus will be given the capacity to see the beauty of God in a way that does not consume us. We will be able to see God for who He is, His raw unfiltered beauty available to our naked eyes. Here is how the response to God's beauty will be experienced:

> After this I looked, and there before me was a great multitude that no one could count, from every nation, tribe, people and language, standing before the throne and before the Lamb. They were wearing white robes and were holding palm branches in their hands. And they cried out in a loud voice: "Salvation belongs to our God, who sits on the throne, and to the Lamb." All the angels were standing around the throne and around the elders and the four living creatures. They fell down on their faces before the throne and worshiped God,

saying: "Amen! Praise and glory and wisdom and thanks and honor and power and strength be to our God for ever and ever. Amen!" (Rev. 7:9–12)

Bounty and beauty come together in this transcendent moment of awe! Like a thousand sunsets unfolding simultaneously, God is seen as *the* giver of the wide variety of good things. God is finally seen as the source of all beauty—as that which brings deep, immense mental and emotional satisfaction. Although these verses do not reference the word *beauty*, we know that the people standing before the throne are witnessing beauty (through God's holiness) by their response to God Himself. They are in that trancelike state, captivated by Him, and we know this because of what is elicited from them in God's presence. You see, beauty stirs within us a connection to transcendence. Academic scholar Patrick T. McCormick, in his wonderful work *God's Beauty*, says, "Indeed, the beauty of the kingdom of God is so striking, so arresting, that those who truly see it are captivated and entranced by it. They cannot turn away from it or pull back from its summons."[2]

THE NECESSITY OF BEAUTY FOR FLOURISHING

Since beauty can act as a beacon, it calls us into the story of everything. A lack of beauty can make it very difficult to see God's desire to give us bounty and to begin to seek Him. Eventually, I graduated from college, left our home of poverty, and began doing well in business before going into ministry. I moved to a much nicer part of town, had a home built, and began enjoying the space and safety of the suburbs. I'll never forget those early days, standing on my front porch as the darkness of night fell, seeing the clear black sky speckled with stars. I'll also never forget the odd, uneasy feeling of quiet . . . actually being rattled by the silence of the suburbs. It took me months to adjust to the lack of sound and motion—no sirens, no distant gunfire, no blaring car stereos, just quiet.

Due to a lifetime of being conditioned for survival, I was rattled by the quiet because there were no predictable sights and sounds for me to process my experience. For an urban guy from Detroit, the quiet and darkness made me feel unsafe, unsettled for quite some time. About a year into my new suburban life, however, I began to acclimate. I had no idea how much I had acclimated to suburbia until I needed to take a trek back into one of the worst parts of Detroit. I pulled onto a street to pick up a friend for a meeting. She was a young, single mom who needed help, and I offered to pick her and her son up for an appointment. I was stopped by the drug dealer on the corner to be checked out. It was a dead-end street, and corner-access homes are considered prime real estate for drug houses, often referred to as a "trap house." After letting him know I wasn't there to buy or use, but to pick up the young mother and her son, I was allowed through. The glares of the six guys on the front porch of the trap house let me know I was no longer an urban insider. I felt and looked awkward and uneasy.

What I had spent a lifetime getting acclimated to was conditioned out of me in just a short year. I remember thinking, *How will this girl's son ever know God in this place?* How can people think about anything other than survival in a place where you have to check in at the trap house every time you come home? There is a worldliness found in excess, indulgence, and greed that prevents people from experiencing the beauty of God. There is, however, another worldliness, one that blinds people from the beauty of God in poverty, insecurity, and want. When we are obsessed with the worries of this world—what we will eat and drink, how we will survive another day, how our children will survive—we can feel like there is a barrier between us and God, a barrier to His beauty and righteousness. This can rob us of our capacity to worship.

Again, we are helped by the scholar McCormick:

> If beauty is that which pleases upon being seen, then the poor see little beauty, for their view is crowded with the unpleasant face of want. In place of a fat bounty that will satisfy our needs, the poor see only a collection of desperate hungers that will not go away and cannot be met. There is not enough food, water, clothing, shelter, work, or medicine—and not enough money to pay for any of these. And these hungers and shortages scar and disfigure their surroundings and

environments. Streets and alleys in their barrios, ghettos, and slums are dark, filthy, and dangerous, littered with uncollected trash, car wrecks, and potholes. Houses and storefronts are boarded up and windows and street lamps shattered. Schools and grocery stores are fortified like prisons. These overcrowded, polluted, dangerous, and exhausted places are not beautiful. Instead, they are the places shunned by anyone who has access to beauty.[3]

I had a new access to a certain kind of beauty in my growing wealth, and I was not only acclimating to it but also beginning to shun the very places that used to be familiar to me. Beauty is one way people witness the wonder of God's presence. Beautiful actions give people, particularly the poor, a unique opportunity to enter into the bounty of God.

By now you may have noticed that part of what we've been doing is the hard work of vocabulary. In order to participate in a new and different kind

Community: *Peoples meaningfully connected to one another because of a common experience, set of ideals or vision, and/or hope for the future.*

of reality, the story of everything, we need to learn and lean into new ideas, firefly ideas like bounty, beauty, righteousness, and a fuller understanding of community. This can be a bit daunting, and

I've introduced new words and new definitions of some very old words. Throughout this book have been callouts highlighting these vocabulary words, and at the end of this book, Appendix B brings all these callouts together in one place. Before moving forward, it may be helpful to skim this chart in order to understand what I'm about to say regarding the relationship between beauty and bounty.

Beauty is essential to bounty. Without beauty, we can't experience righteousness. Let me pause briefly and say, part of the reason why we've looked at so many places in the Bible is because we can't understand firefly ideas like beauty and righteousness without God's Word. The Bible tells us what righteousness looks like and feels like, how we are made right and how we can do right. The Bible teaches us the secrets to accessing bounty in bounty-less places and the Bible tells us the story of where Beauty came from and how we should respond to it. The Holy Spirit is the one who takes the truth of the Bible and connects our story with the great story being told throughout time. As important as beauty and righteousness are, we would not know these ideas or experience them without the Holy Spirit working through God's story—the Bible. Having said that, beauty is, in fact, an access point to the story of everything. Caring for those simple bushes introduced me to my first steps into the story of everything. The beauty effect connects us with who we were meant to be, with others, and with God Himself! Beauty expands our soul, creating a capacity to enter into transcendent ideas like love, hope, and joy. Beauty is meant to draw us into worship.

Worship is the right response to beauty. This is indeed how we were created to respond. It is natural to our true humanity, but it is not natural to our current humanity. The proper response to all beauty is to worship the source of the beauty, not the sub-expressions of beauty. We shouldn't worship the sun, but the source of the sun's fire. We shouldn't worship the snow, but He who spun it into being. This is indeed how we were created to respond. It is natural to our true humanity, but it is not natural to our current humanity. Beauty beckons us to worship, and we can either worship the expression of beauty itself or we can worship the source. All expressions of beauty are spiritual artifacts, glimpses of a better world breaking into our world that is now: a world of ugliness, death, and despair. Beauty is powerful because of this—it is like a lush row of bushes amidst a burned and brittle world. This contrast and the wonder it inspires in us tempts us to worship the expression instead of the source . . . to marvel at mountains, waterfalls, sunsets, and fireflies without connecting in worship with the One who created such wonders.

GETTING READY TO DO BEAUTY

What would it look like to repaint our lives, our communities, our world with beauty? Caring for bushes in

Worship is the right response to beauty. The proper response to all beauty is to worship the source of the beauty, not the sub-expressions of beauty. We shouldn't worship the sun, but the source of the sun's fire. We shouldn't worship the snow, but He who spun it into being.

#dosomethingbeautiful

the ghetto isn't going to change much, but it is a small illustration of the power beauty has to "do something." It is amazing how beautification that points to God can have an affect on evil, suffering, injustices, hopelessness, and isolation.

Beauty is at the core of living righteously, experiencing the bounty we were made for. In this we see how righteousness and beauty are intertwined. You cannot have righteousness without beauty, and you cannot have beauty without righteousness. Beauty should produce righteousness in us, and righteousness in us should demonstrate itself in expressions of beauty. One will always be incomplete without the other. A world made truly beautiful is by definition a world made right, and a world made right is a beautiful world indeed. The greatest expression of this is worship, not of a beautiful person or object but of the true source of all beauty: God Himself. A world made beautiful is a world of worship-filled bounty.

Experiencing beauty should lead us to action, to create beautiful things that stand as a sign in a world of ugliness, despair, and death. There is a causal relationship between all of these ideas. Righteousness, beauty, and community are interdependent ideas, as we will see in the chapters to come. Anyone can "do beauty," but beauty in its truest and fullest form comes from righteousness and produces righteousness. We cannot "do beauty" without "doing righteousness," and vice versa. My simple row of bushes was itself beautiful, but it did not change the choking smells of toxic waste, the danger of violent drug dealers, or the isolation of crack addicts in the trap houses on the street. My bushes were powerless to right these wrongs and give me and those around me the experienced reality of God's righteousness.

Now let's stop for a second and look at how all this relates to the beautiful thing that Jesus did. This is where Jesus comes back into view in a fantastic way. Theologians use the word *atonement*. Atonement at its most basic level means to make one with another.[4] The word is used to describe what the death of Jesus accomplished in creating peace and acceptability between us and God. What is so awe-inspiring about the atoning work of Jesus' death on the cross is that it is a paradox. In death Jesus accomplished something beautiful, and in doing so He provided the bounty that comes from righteousness. There is a duality of good and bad news in the death of Jesus that shows a major contour in the story of everything. Pastor, poet, and dreamer Louie Giglio helps us see that when he says,

> The Cross is not simply legend or story. It occurred at a real place, at a real moment in time, where the Son of the living God—*I AM* in human form—suffered and died. From a human vantage point, the day Jesus died was easily the worst day on earth. Everything that could have gone wrong went wrong. The innocent was accused. Justice was skewed. A mob went wild. Soldiers drove nails through His hands and feet.

His agony was great, as for hours He struggled to breathe. In the end, the sky turned black and, feeling alone and abandoned, Jesus died. . . .

Yet God was not absent that day. He was very much at work, accomplishing something bigger than any of us could have conceived if we were standing in the moment.[5]

The atonement is not just a moment of injustice and suffering but a major piece to a much larger narrative that involves us and God and this world and the world to come!

It's even better than magic. By death, Jesus brought life. By something unjust, justice was established. The death of the Son of God on the cross is the ultimate expression of beauty even in its unfiltered grotesquery, because in it we see the profound extent of the love God has for us. The death of Jesus reveals God's beauty *and* righteousness and is itself the greatest touchpoint for our awe-filled, transcendent

Sacrifice: *To surrender or give up something for the sake of another person, on behalf of an ideal or commitment, or to attain a greater benefit.*

connection with Him through worship. The worship in Revelation 7 is inspired by the sacrifice the "Lamb of God" made on the cross to establish a world made right and beautiful, a world that will come to pass fully at the end of the great story of God!

Before we consider creating beauty, we recognize that a beautiful world is not an end in itself. The greatest form of beauty is God, and the greatest action of beauty on our part is the worship of God. A world made beautiful and righteous is full of a wide variety of good things given freely, and we will see it only imperfectly in this life. That kind of world is a world where God is at the center, receiving the highest expression of beauty for His beauty: worship. A world made right is a world where all have access to the source of beauty, to God Himself. We can plant bushes, paint houses, and sit in front of beautiful sunsets our entire lives, but if we want to truly experience a world made beautiful, we need to spread the good news of the beauty of God and our need for His redemption through Christ to as many people as we possibly can. Any effort to change our lives and our world without God will always be incomplete. God is made known through actions of beauty and righteousness. All this comes into focus in Ephesians 2:8–10:

> For it is by grace you have been saved, through faith—and this is not from yourselves, it is the gift of God—not by works, so that no one can boast. For we are God's handiwork, created in Christ Jesus to do good works, which God prepared in advance for us to do.

We cannot change ourselves or the world by ourselves; we are saved by faith in Jesus Christ. We are, however, saved to do "good works," works of beauty and righteousness. This is what it means to live into the story of everything.

For us to live into the story of everything, we need to "do beauty" and "do righteousness" by knowing God and making Him known. This is where evangelism gets a bad rap. We typically think of evangelism as a salesmanship effort to convince people that they should live and believe a certain set of truths. Evangelism is rather an expression of beauty that reveals the source of beauty because it is the telling of the story of righteousness. It tells us how we can all have access to God's bounty through Jesus' atoning work on the cross. As someone who loves to tell others about Jesus, I find myself feeling like I'm telling people about an amazing painting, an intense galactic meteor shower, or a sun-drenched lake in July.

Think about how you get excited to share good news that pops up on your social media feed. When we get a tweet, an Instagram post, or a Snapchat video of someone announcing that they are engaged, having their first child, getting their first great job, or buying a home, we can't help but "like," "share," "re-post," or simply turn to the person next to us and say, "LOOK AT THIS!" Telling other people about Jesus should be so much better than re-posting a great recipe for the best-ever triple fudge brownies. It should even be more exciting than a gender reveal pregnancy photo or engagement picture. Sharing, liking, and re-posting the gospel is an act of beauty that can change us and change those around us. Evangelism should be like that. It should be normal and natural, like sharing the best news ever. The great news is that as we share Jesus, we find ourselves touched by His beauty each and every time. Talking about Jesus isn't just good for the people who hear. It's good for you too.[6] I don't feel like I'm mechanically moving through some rote gospel outline even when I am. I feel like I'm trying to express a light from another world, an expression of beauty and wonder that is hard to put into words. Evangelism is like that. It is a beautiful thing, making known the bounty of God and inviting people to know the person of Jesus for themselves!

Evangelism in this sense is really how we make the world beautiful and right, because it gives people access to God Himself. In Inkster, I bent in that toxic air. My knees were bruised at the end of that crispy summer after my best attempts to care for my mom's bushes. In the end, I managed to keep a small portion of the ugly world around me at bay and managed to open my heart to something new. Even with this, however, I was still missing the one essential ingredient to make me and my world right— Jesus Christ. Without Jesus we cannot know beauty or righteousness. He showed them to us when He walked the earth, and He's coming back someday to put everything right once again. This is where doing something beautiful comes into view.

CHAPTER 4

DO SOMETHING BEAUTIFUL

"You should say anything important you might have to say now, because we aren't sure your wife is going to make it." My wife, Jodi, was in the hospital, delivering our second child, when the doctor spoke these words to me. These words echoed in my ears because they were the same ones I heard just two years earlier when my wife delivered our first child, also on the brink of death. Both of our biological children were born ten weeks early and at just over two pounds, and in both cases I was told to say my goodbyes, with no assurances that my wife or children would make it through the operation.

In this second near-death operation, the nurses stood in the hallway staring at me to see what my reaction would be. Jodi's family sat quietly praying nearby, and I, again, bent over Jodi's bed to whisper secret words of comfort and blessing. I prayed with her, not knowing if my wife or child would come out of the operating room alive. After this second time, after Jodi and my daughter came home, we began to succumb to the realization that we would never bear another child. It was devastating for Jodi as she always dreamed of having more children. She threw herself into mothering our two healthy, growing children, not knowing that we were just at the beginning of a journey, not the end.

Often in our lives we get to a point where we feel we have no options, where the finality of finances or health or a relationship seems hopeless. Then something happens. There is a twist in the plot and we begin to realize we have a second chance, a new and unforeseen chapter, a wave of new life. We feel as though life is finished as a divorce is finalized, a dream of sports greatness dies, a hard-fought business closes, or a scholarship is lost. In these places of hopelessness, however, something often turns and shifts. Sometimes something happens that is so far beyond what we could have ever imagined, and a new chapter is born. For those who have been made right with God by the beauty of Jesus' death on the cross, a "resurrection factor" repeatedly plays itself out in our lives. This does not always mean that things work out or have a happy ending—not at all. Death is death, sorrow is sorrow, but God is in the business of making beauty rise from ashes and good things emerge after everything seems lost. This is one of the major threads in the story of everything.

THE DEATH OF A DREAM

Growing up, I never dreamed of children. In fact, before I met Jodi I was sure I did not want to have any. Because of my initial lack of desire for kids, the realization that we'd never have more was only disturbing to me in that I saw how absolutely devastating it was for Jodi. Jodi, the woman I loved, had come to the end of a lifelong dream. I saw the woman I love face the death of her dreams and begin to live without hope. It was gut-wrenching for me to watch, but having two kids was two more than I ever thought I'd have, so I was good. For Jodi, however, the realization that we were done having children before she was even twenty-six years old was a death.

In that death Jodi had no choice but to embrace what seemed to be the inevitable—she would need to dream another dream. Loss, pain, death, despair— these are the opposite of beauty and bounty, but Jodi and I have come to realize over and over again that for us, a "resurrection factor" often plays itself out in God's story. Sometimes this works out in ways that are easy, fun, and pleasant, but often the resurrection factor comes through in ways that are like death, ravaging our joy and calling us to deep dependence on God. The things that look hopeless in our lives are

*The things that look
hopeless in our lives
are often used as an
opportunity for God to
show up and bring life
out of death, bounty and
beauty out of the ashes,
and allow us to dream
another dream.*

———————

#dosomethingbeautiful

often used as an opportunity for God to show up and bring life out of death, bounty and beauty out of the ashes, and allow us to dream another dream. This is how the story of everything works, as we found out in the next chapter of Jodi's dream.

We were a few years into the realization that we'd never have another child when a new chapter opened through adoption. Adoption was the furthest thing from my heart and mind, but as God opened that door to bring us our third child, I had a front-row seat to the resurrection factor in Jodi's life. Here is a brief snapshot of that chapter from Jodi's perspective:

> We adopted our daughter Gabby before her first birthday. She is now eight and recently asked me to tell her the story of how she got her name while driving in the car. It's such a great story and though I had told it to her before, as I told it this time I was reminded of how hard the process was and how difficult it is to trust God with a situation that seems hopeless.
>
> I really wanted to adopt a baby, but York did not. At the time, I had been meditating on Zephaniah 3:17, "The Lord your God is with you, the Mighty Warrior who saves." I kept meditating on the fact that God is mighty to save and that He had the power to change our hopeless situation. I thought that He is mighty to change hearts and will either change my heart in order to be content with having only two children or change York's heart to desire more children. It wasn't long after that, around January 2009, that I began to give in to the reality that York's heart was not going to change and that it was

likely I who was going to have to change. I was devastated.
I once again found myself praying, asking God to take away
my desire to adopt. During this time of prayer, however, I
sensed Him telling me, "Gabby is the answer." Now, at this
time I was providing in-home childcare for our neighbor's
daughter, Gabby. Instead of asking God what He meant, I
just concluded on my own that the answer was that we would
never adopt and that taking care of Gabby or other people's
kids or simply serving other young moms was going to be the
answer to fulfilling the deep void I felt. I felt some sadness
but determined to be content.

I began to live into the reality that adoption was a closed
path for several months after this encounter with God, that is,
until June 2010. Mary, a friend of ours who had walked some
of our journey with us, sent York a Facebook message asking
if we were still interested in adopting. Mary shared that they
had a baby girl who was going to be adoptable soon and
thought we would be a good family for her. York reluctantly
showed me the message and asked what I thought. I was
cautiously excited and told him that I wanted to meet the
baby. He sent the message back to Mary to see if we could
meet her that day. She said yes and, providing a little
more detail about the baby's situation, concluded her final
Facebook message with these words, "By the way, her name is
Gabby." Right then and there I knew that this was enough for
God to move York forward, to believe that this was the child
that God had for us. What's more is that God had given me
Gabby's name around the time that she was *conceived*. God
knew her name before her own birth mother did and He *gave*

it to us as a promise even though I was too stupid to know it. And that would have been an amazing story even if it ended there, but there was more.

God provided a child and her name *and* York's heart was changed! We were moving forward. Because God always does immeasurably more than we can even ask or imagine, it doesn't end there, however. As the adoption was getting finalized, Gabby moved in with us. Before the process was final, we needed to decide on her "forever" name. Of course, there was NO WAY that we were changing her first name, but we needed a middle name. We loved Rae because it means female sheep. Two reasons we loved the meaning of female sheep . . . one, Gabby had a little lamb "lovie" (stuffed animal/blanket) that she treasured and snuggled and was always with her. Second, we truly believe, based on her story, that God watched over her and protected her like a shepherd with a lamb. She was His little lamb and He was the Good Shepherd who protected her and brought her to Mary and then to us. It got me wondering what Gabriella meant. When I looked it up, I immediately teared up as I read the words "God is my might" or "God is mighty." I just could not believe it—the very theme of Zephaniah 3:17 that I had been meditating on when I yielded my heart to God's will!

He is an amazing God who heard my prayers and not only gave me the child of my dreams but also gave her a name that answered the cry of my heart and confirmed the claims that I was clinging to. He reminded us that YES, He is mighty and her name will serve as a reminder all the days of our lives. I am forever grateful for God's goodness and for

His faithfulness in even the "little things" like a name that reminds us of His power. I am amazed at His mighty miracles, the sound of His voice, and His love for His little lamb.

Jodi's dream had died. There seemed to be no further chapter to the story until God stepped in and did something beautiful.

THE COST OF BEAUTY

Remember, the sterile definition of beauty refers to the right proportion and alignment of attributes in something or someone that brings deep emotional and/or mental pleasure to the beholder. When God does something beautiful, however, it is often disproportionate, out of alignment with our expectations, and can frequently bring deep pain or struggle before we realize what He is doing or, in Jodi's case, what He had done. There is almost always a price to pay for God's actions of beauty. While Jodi's dream was resurrected, I myself began the painful struggle of receiving God's blessing in Gabby. I am seven years older than my wife, and I did not want to have another child. I feared the financial, emotional, and relational strain another child would have on me and our home. Little did I know that Gabby would not come with a burden, but a blessing.

God's act of beauty in bringing Gabby into my life was incredible and I can't imagine life without her now. At the time, however, all I saw was the cost. I saw new seasons of soiled diapers and burp cloths stained with spit-up. I saw less food, less money, less travel, less everything. Little did I know Gabriella was coming to us with her own blessing from her heavenly Father. She would not drain our home; she would fill it with new life and laughter. There is a cost in doing something beautiful and receiving something beautiful, but the cost pales in comparison to the blessings that arise from doing what God tells us to do. It took me some time to untangle the ugly reasons that I had never wanted children, let alone a third child through adoption. The end result, however, was a blessing of joy and greater bounty in my life. Doing something beautiful doesn't always *feel* beautiful. For me, opening my heart to kids was a painful process, but I found out pretty quickly that *it wasn't about me*— it was about Gabby and God's desire to bless her with a forever mom and dad who were "all in" for her good, who loved her unconditionally as their own.

Doing something beautiful is not like consuming beautiful things. We know all too well how to consume beauty. We "take in" an art show, allow music to wash over us, bathe in the beauty of a park, or marvel at hummingbirds and butterflies in a lush garden. Easy! It is easy and immediately pleasurable to consume beauty, but it is quite another thing to do something beautiful or be the recipient of something beautiful.

You see, doing something beautiful demands something from us. It creates the necessity of worship; it brings a holy hush. Beauty separates the ugly parts of ourselves from the light, allowing righteousness to flourish within and around us. God brought a painful process into my life when my wife's dream was resurrected, but now I can say honestly it was a process of beauty that has produced worship in my heart!

CHANGED BY BEAUTY

If the story of everything has a subplot, it is that transformation comes through the painful process of receiving God's beauty, which often makes us whole through pain. When we experience beauty, we are changed. Change, no matter how wonderful, always comes at a cost. When God does something beautiful, there is a cost, a price that both He and we pay. One of the things that turns people off from church is how rare it is to find anyone who is willing to pay the price for a truly beautiful life. There are many Christians who give everything to God, but there are also so many who barely pay anything at all for their story! In the story of everything, everyone pays a price, but it seems that many religious people want to be immune to this, as if a life of ease and comfort ought to be their birthright. Entire theologies try to support this assumption. Unfortunately, this assumption is the practiced norm of the majority of Christians today. The late philosopher-scholar Dallas Willard put it this way:

> Consumer Christianity is now normative. The consumer Christian is one who utilizes the grace of God for forgiveness and the services of the church for special occasions, but

does not give his or her life and innermost thoughts, feelings, and intentions over to the kingdom of the heavens. Such Christians are not inwardly transformed and not committed to it.[1]

Giving our innermost thoughts, feelings, and intentions over to God is the only way to receive and benefit from the beauty of true transformation. By design, transformation comes through death—death of self-interest, death of expectations, or death of control.

We certainly see this in the beauty of the cross. The death Jesus paid to give us the second chance we didn't deserve was an act of costly beauty. In His case, it was an actual, literal death. God is in the business of "doing beauty," and as we live into the story of everything, we are invited by God to "do beauty" too. Doing beauty is costly, risky, and life changing! When we experience or consume beauty, the proper response is to *do* beauty, to re-create it in our world and in the lives of others.

Artists naturally create beauty from the inspiration they get from beauty. Great artists can perceive and point out beauty where there seems to be none, even in the ashes of pain and death, loss and struggle. I believe that God is the greatest artist. I see this in dancing fields of light, foaming ocean bluffs, and the face of my three precious children, Kiren, Addison, and Gabby. God doesn't need to look to beauty to create beauty; He Himself is the source and from Him can only come beautiful things. For us, doing beauty is more art than science; it is about perceiving the difference between what is and what should be and then attempting to respond by painting a preferred alternate reality.

Jesus knew how to do beauty well, with excellence, to make joy rise from sorrow. In Mark 5:21–43 we read of two life-giving miracles. This story is long, but I want you to consider it as one of the best examples of doing beauty in the complexity and difficulty of broken people and broken circumstances:

> When Jesus had again crossed over by boat to the other side of the lake, a large crowd gathered around him while he was by the lake. Then one of the synagogue leaders, named Jairus, came, and when he saw Jesus, he fell at his feet. He pleaded earnestly with him, "My little daughter is dying. Please come and put your hands on her so that she will be healed and live." So Jesus went with him.
>
> A large crowd followed and pressed around him. And a woman was there who had been subject to bleeding for twelve years. She had suffered a great deal under the care of many doctors and had spent all she had, yet instead of getting better she grew worse. When she heard about Jesus, she came up behind him in the crowd and touched his cloak, because she thought, "If I just touch his clothes, I will be healed." Immediately her bleeding stopped and she felt in her body that she was freed from her suffering.
>
> At once Jesus realized that power had gone out from him.

He turned around in the crowd and asked, "Who touched my clothes?"

"You see the people crowding against you," his disciples answered, "and yet you can ask, 'Who touched me?'"

But Jesus kept looking around to see who had done it. Then the woman, knowing what had happened to her, came and fell at his feet and, trembling with fear, told him the whole truth. He said to her, "Daughter, your faith has healed you. Go in peace and be freed from your suffering."

While Jesus was still speaking, some people came from the house of Jairus, the synagogue leader. "Your daughter is dead," they said. "Why bother the teacher anymore?"

Overhearing what they said, Jesus told him, "Don't be afraid; just believe."

He did not let anyone follow him except Peter, James and John the brother of James. When they came to the home of the synagogue leader, Jesus saw a commotion, with people crying and wailing loudly. He went in and said to them, "Why all this commotion and wailing? The child is not dead but asleep." But they laughed at him.

After he put them all out, he took the child's father and mother and the disciples who were with him, and went in where the child was. He took her by the hand and said to her, *"Talitha koum!"* (which means "Little girl, I say to you, get up!"). Immediately the girl stood up and began to walk around (she was twelve years old). At this they were completely astonished. He gave strict orders not to let anyone know about this, and told them to give her something to eat.

Besides Jesus, there are two major players in this story and they couldn't be more different. The leader of the synagogue was a respected member of the community, a person of stature. From people's perspective, he was "worthy" of Jesus' intervention in his daughter's illness. This man's sorrow was real; with the child's death came the death of the dream of being a father to his little girl. This man was desperate, and so he came to Jesus because he believed in and sought a miracle from Jesus. He knew that if Jesus could just lay His hands on his child, she would live. Jesus saw the synagogue leader's faith and agreed to go with him, but along the way Jesus got deterred by our second character who, from the people's perspective, was not "worthy" of Jesus' intervention.

On the way to save the little girl of a righteous man, an unclean woman on the list of unembraceables seemingly stole the resurrection power of Jesus from the little girl. This woman was an outcast in her day as she suffered from what was very likely a perpetual menstruation, making her socially and religiously "unclean." She was unembraceable particularly by the very law this synagogue leader preached, taught, and enforced week in and week out. Like the synagogue leader, however, she believed that Jesus was the answer to her sorrow. This woman had spent all she had on medical treatment but only continued to suffer and grow worse. She was not just sick in body; she was as good as dead socially and religiously. She could not visit family or friends and she certainly couldn't go to this man's synagogue. This woman was isolated, alone in her suffering. She and the daughter of the synagogue leader were both in need of healing. Believing Jesus was able to end her sorrow, she snuck up behind Him and grabbed hold of His cloak—and was made well.

THERE'S ENOUGH JESUS TO GO AROUND

Although there is so much to say about this event, what is important right now is this: it appears as if this unclean, unwanted woman has literally stolen the resurrection blessing of Jesus away from the synagogue leader, because at the exact same time, his daughter was reported dead. Or at least this is how a scarcity mindset about God works: we think that there is only so much beauty to go around, that God's bounty has an expiration date, and we had better get it while the getting is good.

However, when we find our place in the story of everything, we find a "kingdom abundance," a bounty at play. *This is what is so incredible about Jesus—He is not changing the fiber of our world into something it has never been; He is restoring what always should have been.* The little girl should never have been sick in the first place. The woman should never have been sick or ostracized. God made a world that was beautiful and right: it had no sickness and pain and it was meant to stay that way. The miracle of the story of everything is that it is a restoration of what was lost, as Pastor Tim

Keller says in *The Reason for God*,

> We modern people think of miracles as the suspension of the natural order, but Jesus meant them to be the restoration of the natural order. The Bible tells us that God did not originally make the world to have disease, hunger, or death in it. . . . Jesus's miracles are not just a challenge to our minds, but a promise to our hearts, that the world we all want is coming.[2]

The lack of understanding about kingdom abundance is at play in this story about two desperate people who believe there is only so much Jesus to go around. The synagogue leader came to Jesus for healing, but Jesus' healing power went out from Him to this woman, and now the man's daughter has died. This woman was declared healed after telling the truth, her faith in Jesus making her well. For her, there was finally a new chapter of joy in her life, but not so for the synagogue leader. I can imagine the simultaneous tears of joy from her juxtaposed by the weeping of this father whose daughter is now dead.

At this point, however, Jesus chose to enter into the synagogue leader's pain, to enter into the context of suffering and sorrow. Jesus went to his house, which was now a place of weeping and death. There, Jesus did something beautiful. He actually raised the girl from the dead! The synagogue leader had hoped for a healing and succumbed to the fact that his daughter would never be healed but had died. Instead of a healing, however, he got a resurrection! Although

*Great artists can
perceive beauty where
there seems to be none,
even in the ashes
of pain and death,
loss and struggle.
I believe that God is
the greatest artist.*

———————

#dosomethingbeautiful

there is absolutely no biblical reason to think that this happened, I like to imagine the woman healed from her chronic menstruation sitting in the front row of the synagogue on the following Sabbath with the leader's daughter sitting on her lap. Wouldn't that have been a beautiful thing to see?!

LESSONS FROM THE STORY OF EVERYTHING

The parallelism in this passage is intentional for Mark. It is what biblical scholars refer to as a *pericope*—here we have two different stories with similar contours that demonstrate principles about the story of everything. It is the story of two resurrections, two stories of faith. One told from a place of access and privilege; one from a place of desperation and ostracism. In both cases, Jesus was enough. This story teaches us three profound things about doing beauty well.

First, God does beautiful things in places of ugliness, where the weeping is not pretty, in the snot- and tear-filled places where there seems to be no hope at all. In Jewish culture, this woman in menstruation was as untouchable as the dead body of the little girl—an irony that is almost certainly intended in Mark's gospel. They are both hopeless, untouchable, unembraceable.

Second, Jesus brings hope where, by worldly standards, there is none. No doctor and no amount of money could heal the woman, and no mourning or crying could ever have brought the little girl back to life. Only Jesus could. You see, God does beautiful things in the lives of people who have depleted their resources, who are suffering, who have for all intents and purposes died.

Third, in this story we see Jesus entering into places of pain and chaos. He stops in the midst of the pushing crowd and recognizes the personhood of the unclean woman. Notice that Jesus says, "*Daughter*, your faith has healed you." To the people, the sick woman was just another unembraceable person, but to Jesus she was a daughter of God. He saw her, she was beautiful, she mattered. Likewise, Jesus also entered the bedroom of a dead body amidst weeping and pain, and He was able to stoop down in the commotion of the crowd because of His perspective. This is where doing complex and costly beauty becomes practical for us.

As you follow Jesus, I want to challenge you to have a perspective and posture that is against the norm in our culture—to begin to see places of pain and loss as opportunities to enter into the story of everything for yourself. Embrace complexity, embrace pain, embrace the beauty that comes from adaptation and adjustment and discomfort. You know how the world says "play it safe," "take care of yourself," and "don't get too involved"? I want to challenge you to do the opposite and watch the magic that comes from the mess. Your suspicions are right. Our American Dream or fantasy of personal wealth, personal safety, and personal indulgence is not the way to experience God's best for us; it is the way of slow death. The way to life is in following Jesus into the crowd, trusting Him in the bedroom of weeping, for in following Him there we find the beauty of love.

How do we do beauty then? We join God where the need is great. We do the things Jesus would do in the presence of need. One of the reasons many churchgoing people get stagnant in their faith is that they don't go where God wants them to go and they don't do the things Jesus would do. They spend their lives avoiding pain, discomfort, and awkwardness. People are wanting, hurting, aching for someone to enter their story, but here's the secret: the best version of ourselves unfolds when we are on the edge, doing risky things with God and for people!

While we *should* do things simply because they are the right things to do, we often don't. Now, to be sure, nothing that we *do* makes us right. The Bible is clear: righteousness is a gift from God—we don't earn it. Ephesians 2:8–9 reminds us, "For it is by grace you have been saved, through faith—and this is not from yourselves, it is the gift of God—not by works, so that no one can boast." Righteousness is what righteous people do; it is not the means to their righteousness. When righteous people do righteousness, then we "live into" who we were created to be—Ephesians 2:10 goes on to say, "For we are God's handiwork, created in Christ Jesus to do good works, which God prepared in advance for us to do." The things we are supposed to do, that we are duty-bound to do, are also the very things that expose God's blessing in our lives. As we do right because it is right to do, we experience something beautiful . . . transformation!

DOING BEAUTY AMONG THE CHILDREN OF OUR DAY

About two years after we adopted Gabby, a relative said to me privately, "It sure is a nice thing you've done for that little girl, bringing her into your family."

By this time I had come to know the secret, however, so I responded with a laugh, "No, you have it backwards. God brought her into our lives and home to bless us! I get to take care of God's daughter and I've gotten much more than she has gotten from me."

I believe one of the greatest and most beautiful things we can do with the resources we have in this moment of history is to care for the daughters and sons of God. Children who have been abandoned and neglected, thrown away and labeled unembraceable are all around us. There seems to be no hope, and the crisis is getting worse by the day. One of the most complex acts of beauty we can do, if we are able, is to care for the girls and boys who are as good as dead, those who are living the unembraceable life of a foster child. While we might never refer to foster children as unclean, the statistics are clear—most of them are as good as dead.

The drug rates, suicide rates, incarceration rates, homelessness rates, and disease rates among children who grew up up in the foster care system demonstrate that a modern-day leper colony is rising among us. We can do something about this, but it requires a dedication to complex beauty and a firm belief in the "resurrection factor." The good news is this: Jesus is enough! If you are able, I beg you for your sake and theirs, take your home, your gifts, your time, and invest in the lives of children in foster care! You can create bounty in the lives of children who have been secretly placed on the list of unembraceables—our foster care system is absolutely filled with them. Now, not everyone can do this, of course. Perhaps you are a college student or a single person just getting started on your career. You can participate in this area of great need by supporting those who are on the front lines as foster parents. Maybe you can open your church to provide foster care training for others. Maybe you can organize a clothing and toy drive in your community for a local foster care agency. There are many ways to care for and love the forgotten children of our day.

Of particular concern in this moment of history is the impact the opioid epidemic has had in elevating the number of children in foster care. Through heroin and prescription drug addiction, families are being torn apart in every place and among every class and people group. We are living in a crisis moment that is getting considerably worse by the day. There are easily more than half a million children living in foster care right now and the numbers are climbing fast. Children and teenagers are being removed by child protective services in increasing numbers and being placed in a foster care system that was already overloaded and has now surpassed its breaking point. Even without the opioid epidemic, precious children who are as good as dead fill facilities and float from

Risk: *The state of being exposed to uncertainty and, by extension, certain dangers associated with such uncertainty.*

home to home. They are like this daughter, like this menstruating woman—desperate for something beautiful. Caring for these children as licensed foster care providers is one way we can do beauty in all its complexity. We can be the means of someone else's second chance, their exposure to God's love. Adopting through foster care where possible is a powerful way to do beauty in the lives of desperate children in a time of national and personal crisis. I, for one, long for a day when the front pews of churches in America are filled with little girls and boys, sitting on the laps of people who have themselves experienced the resurrection of Jesus Christ. This is *not* easy. It is not for the faint of heart. And it is a long journey, but it's worth it!

What do you long to see? Maybe your longing, your ache for a world made right, revolves around caring for a shut-in, elderly person. Perhaps it revolves around incarcerated persons, trafficking survivors, teen mothers trapped in dead-end-street lives. Fostering and adoption are just one way to do something beautiful, but there are many others. Instead of listing the many ways we can do something beautiful, I want to say that doing beauty is best done where the commotion is high, despair has set in, and the body of death seems like the end of someone's dream. Look around you. Listen to the needs and consider. Enter in. Take the risk of doing beauty where you can. Here are some questions to help get you started.

DO SOMETHING BEAUTIFUL:

1. Where is sorrow impacting your immediate community?

2. What is the source of the sorrow in your immediate community?

3. What is needed to meet the needs of those who are suffering?

4. What would beauty look like to those who are suffering around you?

5. What one beautiful thing can you do to enter into the sorrow of those around you?

6. What will doing something beautiful cost you?

7. What can you do to prepare to pay the price for doing something beautiful?

CHAPTER 5

A WORLD BROUGHT TOGETHER

Waiting anxiously with our hastily homemade cereal-box viewers in hand, I sat with my two daughters on the back patio as day turned to night during the Great American Eclipse of 2017. For the hour before the eclipse, we watched the country brought together in this celestial spectacle via television. Over and over again, from city to city my girls and I witnessed something incredible. We watched as the world was brought together around something beautiful.

"Daddy," my seven-year-old asked, "why are the people crying and laughing?" Flickering between shots of the moon eclipsing the sun and sprinkled between meteorologist explanations were hundreds or thousands of people weeping and/or laughing in the background of nearly every shot. Gabby, my seven-year-old, wanted to know why people were having such a visceral reaction to the eclipse. She had never seen such a human response to anything like this before. I thought for a while about how to answer her question as I was managing to get my own feelings under control. I finally answered her, "Gabby, all these people are experiencing something *together*. They are so happy that they get to see this beautiful event that they are overwhelmed." In typical seven-year-old form, Gabby's response was simply, "Well that's dumb. Can I have some lunch?" What was lost on Gabby in that moment was how powerful a shared experience can be.

There is a power in the awe-inspiring expressions of the universe, a power amplified through our shared human experience. A shared experience brings people together like nothing else! We watched the clock and the sky as day started to turn to night at our own house. We knew finally it was our time as the distant blue sky stretched green and pale and crickets began to chirp. Though we had 100 percent cloud cover at our home for the few minutes the eclipse came to our town, my girls and I sat huddled together, makeshift cereal-box viewers in hand, and joined the rest of America. We never saw the eclipse ourselves because of the clouds, but I'll never forget holding Gabby tight while quietly smiling and winking at Addison, my fifteen-year-old. As we sat in darkness together on the back patio, along with the rest of the country, we experienced firsthand the power of a shared experience. That memory will likely be with my girls and me the rest of our lives. Clouds, crickets,

and cereal boxes brought us together as we sat with
America during the Great American Eclipse of 2017.

THE THINGS THAT BIND

In the story of everything, many things bind us together.
We have shared experiences around wonder and
beauty but also evil and suffering. There are many
experiences that can bind us together, events where
our shared humanity inspires us to bravery, virtue,
and transparency. A storm on the horizon causes the
sky to stretch green as a different kind of darkness
covers us. New Yorkers and most Americans were
brought together after the darkness of 9/11. During
that darkness, we witnessed brave women and men
risk their lives, sacrifice their resources, and give
themselves to the rescue and recovery process—almost
always for complete strangers.

The story of everything tells us that we are in fact
all bound together. We belong to one another, get joy
from relying on each other, and can't be truly human
without community. Most of the time this is hard to
see in our daily lives. But from time to time the veil
separating our world from the world to come is torn,
and what spills out in things like fireflies, baseball
games, and an eclipse binds us together.

This is another way we know our suspicions are
right, our longings pointing the way to who we were
meant to be and how the world is supposed to be. The
story of everything tells us that God is community and

made us for that community. It also tells us God made a way for that community to happen. Community is formed during these big events, if only for a moment. We feel that longing stirred and so we gasp and smile, wink and nod, laugh and cry. That was really what was at play in the awe, weeping, marveling, and laughter of the Great American Eclipse.

What was so surprising to my seven-year-old was astounding to me as well. In watching the footage of the eclipse, it seemed absolutely normal for complete strangers to openly weep, to burst out in spontaneous laughter, to ooh and ahh at the sun and moon. For just a few minutes, people were brought together by something unusual, something beautiful. What was so awe-inspiring on the day of the eclipse in August 2017 was not just the moon passing before the sun for a few brief moments; it was the event-driven community, the shared experience with large numbers of others. As spectacular as the eclipse was, even for those of us who only saw it on television, the real source of weeping and laughing was that, for a moment, the world was brought together because of something otherworldly.

SHARED EXPERIENCES ARE NOT ENOUGH

Think about what we say after tragedies. It shows us how we're all longing for the community that the story of everything is offering but it only comes in half-glimpses and fast-fading flashes of light. I've witnessed this

phenomenon repeatedly my entire life, but my inter-
pretation is quite different from that of the newscasters
and cultural pundits. Most often, we point to the "*true*
human spirit*," our "shared humanity." We hear things
like, "That's what we would expect from the greatest
city in the world," or after the historic flooding in
Houston, "That's just what Houstonians do."

We want to believe that the weeping, laughing,
heroics, and virtuous actions are the *true* face of
humanity. We think that these positive shared
experiences will one day erase the evil actions of
others or make sense of the greatest natural disasters.
And at some level, we're right. Your suspicions are
right. The story of everything tells us God meant for us
to be this way. True humanity is found in community.
But there's a problem. Not long after the expressions
of joy, love, and kindness experienced under the
eclipse and in the aftermath of helping strangers
in hurricanes, another face of humanity was on full
display. A wealthy and seemingly normal man went on
a shooting spree at a Las Vegas music concert, killing
fifty-eight people and injuring more than five hundred
others. This sniper in Las Vegas emptied hundreds of
rounds into a crowd of thousands; he killed strangers
in the night before killing himself. Isn't this also the
"*true* face" of humanity?

This shared experience also creates a communal
memory. But the fallacy, the great lie we reinforce after
events like these, is that the actions of that sniper are
alien to the true face of humanity. I would disagree.

What disturbs us deep down is not how alien evil is, but how familiar it is to us. In the grotesqueries of the world, we see a version of ourselves glancing back, and we convince ourselves that this is somehow not us, at least not the true us. In fact, evil is all around, but we allow it to masquerade as other things in order to make sense of ourselves and our world. Here we are helped by the wisdom of philosopher Cornelius Plantinga, in his award-winning, must-read *Not the Way It's Supposed to Be: A Breviary of Sin.* He says, "To do its worst, evil needs to look its best. Evil has to spend a lot of time in makeup." He continues, "Vices have to masquerade as virtues—lust as love, thinly veiled sadism as military discipline, envy as righteous indignation, domestic tyranny as parental concern."[1]

Unexplained public expressions of evil just will not do. We domesticate evil, but in the story of everything we see how evil is real and emanates from a power that is well beyond our control. We need to accept the reality of evil and have a better understanding of its source, something the Bible calls sin. We try desperately to avoid this idea of sin, thinking of it as some kind of antique word that used to serve a function in life, like an outhouse before we had indoor plumbing. We always try to make evil about something else, but evil is ultimately about sin. And if sin is real, then all sorts of other aspects of the pseudo-story we've come to believe about ourselves and the world come crashing down. For example, in predictable fashion, just after the Las Vegas massacre, the media turned the conversation from evil to a conversation about gun control. The massacre in Las Vegas is as much about gun control as 9/11 is about airport security—both miss the true heart of the matter. Both are an attempt to rationalize evil and to create distance between us and sin. That doesn't mean there is never a time or place to talk about proper or improper access to guns. This conversation is an important one and needed more and more as our world grows ever darker. However, we must not miss the foundational point—a heart set on evil will do evil regardless of the means.

We just cannot accept the truth that supernatural darkness is at play within us and our world. But it is. Believing this and understanding what to do about it are integral to finding our place in the story of everything. We are not the heroes in the story of everything. Though there is great virtue in doing beauty and righteousness, doing so does not make us heroes. We are more like very sick and injured patients who grope for hope amidst the flickering wreckage and fallout of a bomb-riddled hospital in the middle of a war. We ourselves need tending to, and as we stretch out our hands to assist others just like us, we do not rise above their status—we all are under the power and effects of evil and sin.

Sin and the expressions of sin (evil) are an affront to God's story. Again, Plantinga says, "God hates sin not just because it violates his law but, more substantively, because it violates shalom, because it breaks the peace, because it interferes with the

We always try to make evil about something else, but evil is ultimately about sin. And if sin is real, then all sorts of other aspects of the pseudo-story we've come to believe about ourselves and the world come crashing down.

#dosomethingbeautiful

way things are supposed to be."[2] The true issue at the center of shocking crimes is evil, the evil that is common to us, not an evil that is reserved for snipers and terrorists. What disturbs us most about the Las Vegas sniper was that he was a normal guy. He went on cruises, sent cookies to his mother, and had loving romance and friendships. He was just like us. We are all in the same boat. That deconstructs the fabricated happily-ever-after story of the American Dream. Your suspicions were right all along: something is amiss, there is a tear in our world, and that other world is coming in, shining light and exposing our darkness.

HOPE IS SEEN IN WANTING

The vision of a world brought together is not sustainable simply by our belief that we are better than we really are. It isn't sustainable through shared experiences either, no matter how wonderful they may be. We will never overcome the creeping darkness of a sky stretching green with evil simply through some sense of shared humanity. We can never experience sustained goodness and community in the world without one essential ingredient. The hurricanes move on, the stench of sewage lingers, the federal aid is slow in coming. We see rioting and looting, stealing and hatred too. These are just as true expressions of humanity as the weeping and laughing, the hugs and smiles around our back-patio cereal-box viewers. Yet we long for beauty and righteousness, don't we?

We *wish* it were true that our love would win in the end. The phrase "Love Wins" has come to mean many things for many people, but for all it is an expression of hope. We *want* love to win. We actually desire the best expressions of humanity to be the normative, sustained expressions that will one day win out, don't we? A shared experience of misery, challenge, or suffering beckons us to our true desire—for a world made right and beautiful, a world brought together. This is the heart of humanity that we choose time and time again. We want it and taste it from time to time, and because of it most people are holding out for something more than what we normally experience. Under a dark sky with strangers staring into beauty, giving blood after the killing has ended in Las Vegas, digging through rubble in the aftermath of a terrorist attack—we *want* to be together, we *want* to experience beauty, and we *want* the world to be made right. In the end, while it is not the true face of humanity, something inside of us longs for a righteous and beautiful community, even if we are determined to try and get it ourselves—apart from God. That's because it's what we were made for. But we can't rebuild this on our own; our sin is too big.

Although we may often secretly suspect that the world we long for is not going to materialize, we still want it. It is in this wanting that we find the hope of something greater. During the drought of 1987, as my family lived in fear of gun violence, drugs, and crime, there was an even greater danger in the air. About 7:00

or 8:00 p.m., just like clockwork, a strange and dense stench would fill the streets. The smell was so strong that people often walked with their shirts or jackets pulled up over their faces. Closing the windows never kept the thick smell out, and although no one knew what it was, a great fear from house to house covered our neighborhood.

After years of our living with this predictable stench, a lawyer came knocking on our door and invited us to a meeting where he and our neighbors would talk about a potential lawsuit against an industrial plant down the street. He said he and others believed this plant was intentionally dumping dangerous chemicals into city sewer lines and that the noxious stench was evidence of this. We agreed to come to the meeting; there, our worst fears were realized. Neighbor after neighbor began to share stories of the smells and sicknesses. Several neighbors reported trips to the emergency room and worse. There seemed to be a high number of people with cancers and other life-threatening illnesses. As speculation turned into panic, the lawyer's work was done. In one single meeting he had galvanized a community of complete strangers around a common fear. He had rallied our shared desire for a world made right and beautiful, bringing us together for the purposes of a lawsuit.

The class-action lawsuit lasted years. Several of us, including me, were deposed repeatedly. I'll never forget one deposition as I sat alone with my lawyer across from nine lawyers with expensive briefcases and suits tailored to perfection. I was deposed for nearly nine hours straight with just a brief break for lunch. Question after question attacked the motives of my neighbors, my motives, and the motives of my mother and brothers. The questions were designed to demonstrate that we were just after money, picking an easy target to blame our poverty and suffering on. I stood strong, however, as did the rest of the community, and in the end we settled out of court for millions of dollars. After the huge lawyer fees and the expense of executing a five-year-long case were subtracted, each resident received between just a few thousand dollars and tens of thousands of dollars. We had won the day, or so we thought. After we received our checks, we never saw our champion lawyer again. Within a few years we began to smell that familiar stench of hopelessness as fumes filled the air. We had been brought together in our hope for a better life, but even though "justice" had won that particular day, we quickly went back to being strangers in our shared experience of misery and woe, not much better off than we were before. We needed a better community.

HOPE IS FOUND IN THE HOLY SPIRIT

The proper response to the recurrent evil, hatred, bigotry, and suffering around us should neither be hopelessness nor unrealistic hope in humanity's good. There is "hope in our hope," if it is in the right element.

Now for the essential ingredient, the one thing in this
world that can actually bring us together for good. Just
after Jesus was murdered and had been raised from
the dead, His followers were given a supernatural,
unstoppable, irresistible, binding power for good: the
Holy Spirit. The Spirit of God is the essential ingredient
to creating and sustaining a righteous community that
is capable of establishing the wonder of beauty in a
broken world!

When the Holy Spirit came, He came for good, to
live within those who professed Jesus. This was the
start, the firefly flicker of green over a field of mud
and forgotten corn. The Holy Spirit is Himself the
very source of light and power from that other world,
and He is at the center of the story of everything. As
we learn in the Bible, the Holy Spirit is your guide to
finding your place in the story of everything too, as we
will see. He is the center of the righteous and beautiful
community, a community Jesus promised to establish
through those who would follow Him. As Jesus'
followers gathered, Acts 2 tells us they were filled
with the Spirit and began preaching and teaching
with great authority, with signs and wonders, and as
a result thousands were baptized into the community.
After this happened, we read these words,

> Everyone was filled with awe at the many wonders and signs
> performed by the apostles. All the believers were together
> and had everything in common. They sold property and
> possessions to give to anyone who had need. Every day they

continued to meet together in the temple courts. They broke bread in their homes and ate together with glad and sincere hearts, praising God and enjoying the favor of all the people. And the Lord added to their number daily those who were being saved. (Acts 2:43–47)

The awe that came over America in the eclipse of 2017 lasted for less than three minutes. The Las Vegas sniper rained down death from his perch for ten minutes. *Both worldly awe and worldly suffering lasts for just a short period of time, but God's Spirit-filled community is a sustained community of beauty.* For these new Christians, the awe was ongoing because they were experiencing something right and beautiful in a community powered by the Holy Spirit Himself. They were all together; they shared possessions and looked out for one another. They ate and spent time in one another's homes. They had a missional purpose that drove them to risk and danger, yet they were happy, generous, and thankful. Isn't *that* what you have been hoping for all this time? Isn't *that* something worth pursuing, something worth gambling on, something worth investing in? Don't your longings lead you time and time again back to this same place—a deep, unsatiated desire for a righteous and beautiful community?

Unfortunately, all this might as well be a pink, polka-dotted unicorn, right?! We've already shown we can't craft lasting community on our own. Does such a community really exist? If it did, wouldn't people be selling everything they have, packing up, and moving to be a part of it? Our brushes with this kind of community are just a dim, temporary shadow of what we really want. If we can pay enough money, we can have some of this with strangers on a cruise. When catastrophe hits, we find people to be generous and full of goodwill for a season. Among close friends and family, we spend time eating and visiting one another's homes.

These new Christians, however, were brought together out of something more powerful: their shared experience of the Holy Spirit and their core conviction in the mission of Jesus Christ! This picture in Acts 2 is what Jesus had in mind when He invited His friends to follow Him. He was actually inviting them to a righteous and beautiful community. This Spirit-filled community would then become the way for others all over the world and throughout time to also experience righteousness and beauty. This community was sustainable not because the members were perfect but because they believed in Jesus, and in believing in Jesus they were given the presence of the Spirit of God.

THE RIGHTEOUS AND BEAUTIFUL COMMUNITY IS FILLED WITH IMPERFECT PEOPLE

Believing in Jesus does not make you perfect, but it does give you access to a supernatural power—the Holy Spirit—who is capable of creating sustained change. When the Holy Spirit comes into a person's life as a result of believing in Jesus, radical, life-altering change begins and spans throughout that person's life. It allows you to be truly human. When people who are in the process of being changed come together because of their shared experience and conviction, they don't stop being imperfect. In fact, the more imperfect people you get together, the greater the amplification of their collective imperfections will be. This is part of the reason that so many people have had such a bad experience with collections of Christians in this thing we call the church. We have high expectations of the church but are constantly disappointed, because what we typically experience is something far short of the Acts 2 community of spiritual vibrancy, awe, and togetherness. The Spirit does, however, change people; and changed people, when brought together in the mission of Jesus, end up changing the world! When we believe in Jesus, we are given a supernatural power that changes us and makes the righteous and beautiful community a real possibility. The good news is that when we are made right with God, we become the people of God.

All one has to do is read the rest of the New Testament story to realize that these new Christians were far from perfect. Some members of this new community had sex addictions, struggled with alcohol abuse, had racist and sexist views, mixed their belief in Jesus with false religious practices, and still used people as slaves! They were some of the worst versions of humanity, but something incredible had begun to happen . . . they were filled with a supernatural power. That power had begun to so drastically change them from the inside out that they were envied by outsiders because of their joy, generosity, and community. They weren't perfect, but an irreversible process had begun that would eventually spread to the rest of the planet!

I meet many people who say they will not follow Jesus because they know too many Christians. When I ask for examples, they usually tell me of hypocrisy, spousal abuse, infidelity, and other stories of sin. There are certainly many people who profess Jesus but don't really know Him, yes, but the real trouble is that the true followers of Jesus are often not much better. Porn addiction, struggles with drugs and alcohol, gossiping, bitterness, and anger. These are all the manifestations of the darkness common to every human being. We already know that the Bible calls this darkness *sin*, and it is exactly why we need the Holy Spirit and the righteous and beautiful community—so that we can become well. When people tell me of their examples of awful Christians, I ask them if they think that they themselves are all that much better than those they are talking about. Usually, they admit that they are not, but that they don't pretend to be either.

The real problem many non-Christians have with Christians is that they see Christians as holding out a different standard. Christians are *supposed* to be good, right? I am a sinner. I am also a saint. Both statements are true. I was saved from the eternal consequences of my sin once and for all when I professed Jesus. I am being delivered from sin's power as I am filled with the Holy Spirit and walk in community with others. I will ultimately be saved from sin's presence in the world to come. The great news is that through community with other people who have the Holy Spirit indwelling them, we are, *together*, becoming new! The battle is still being fought. Even though the end result has already been determined, it is critical that we stay engaged and continue to grow in our faith in the context of community.

ONCE YOU'VE EXPERIENCED IT, YOU WILL ALWAYS SEEK IT

Righteousness and beauty are possible in a sustained way in a community that is powered by the Holy Spirit. When I first became a Christian, I experienced first-hand this kind of electric, Spirit-filled community in my local church. For some strange reason, many of my friends at this church had also just become Christians, though almost none of them through the church's ministry. We were all drawn to the church primarily because of the fantastic Bible teaching, but in coming together, we all found so much more. Having just come to know Jesus, we had just received the Holy Spirit, and as a result, we were experiencing that Acts 2 awe, an electric buzz of a red-hot, missional community. Now, among us were racists, struggling alcoholics, people with eating disorders, and porn addicts. We weren't

When the Holy Spirit comes into a person's life as a result of believing in Jesus, radical, life-altering change begins and spans throughout that person's life.

#dosomethingbeautiful

perfect, but we had all experienced the Holy Spirit and we were sure that Jesus was real! This was the first time I had ever experienced anything like that. It was a real and sustained community that has forever marked me.

Nothing in my life has ever compared to the very first time I had an Acts 2 family. Week after week, we met in one another's homes, ate together, sang together, laughed together, and cried together. We dealt with our mess too. We had snot-filled, weeping conversations about race and porn and food and family—we were all in when it came to being honest with our sin and circumstances. As a result, almost all of us became victorious over lifelong struggles and deep-seated pain.

We also lived *missional* lives. We went into the streets of Detroit to do life and mission together and we regularly saw people become Christians through our ministry. Before that time I never believed this kind of community was possible and certainly not possible for someone like me. Being with these people when I first became a Christian was the greatest experience I had ever had, but I naively believed that this community would go on as it was for the rest of my life. My experience was so ongoing and visceral that I was confused when it came to an end. Many of my Christian friends married one another, moved away, and started families. What was once a red-hot, passionate, and Spirit-filled community became friendships separated by time and space. Although I was confused and at times angry that this experience had come to an end, because I had tasted it, I have longed to reproduce it in other places and for other people my entire life.

Knowing that something is possible makes us long for it that much more. I met Jesus and became a Christian. Many people have this same story. Unfortunately, far fewer have known a community of awe, experiencing the wonder of transformation. Fewer still have the kind of community experience in which people sell their goods and put themselves on the line for others as described here in Acts 2. What millions of churchgoing people in America don't realize is that Spirit-filled community is supposed to be so much more. It is supposed to be more like the awe of a great eclipse and the generosity and sacrifice in the aftermath of hurricanes.

Since we've not tasted an Acts 2 community, we settle for a few songs and a good homily, a plastic cup of grape juice and a wafer sliver. We settle for polite Sunday greetings followed by safe family dinners at a nearby family diner. Nothing could be further from the missional community of Jesus, a radical bunch of Spirit-filled people snatched from the stench of ghettos, sexual addiction, alcohol abuse, and cultural arrogance. This kind of community may not be perfect, but I'll trade perfect any day for the awe and joy I had with that first group of Christians! Don't get me wrong, there is much to say about the lifestyle of millions of Christians who are faithfully

living life day by day, reading their Bibles and praying.
Going to church and serving, giving faithfully and
cheerfully, enjoying fellowship and living a chaste
and quiet life—these are also signs of a Spirit-filled
community. One type of living doesn't negate the
other, and both are expressions of the renewing work
of the Spirit. Where the Spirit is bringing new life,
however, out of places of death, that resurrection
power produces a kind of energy that is different and
radical. That radical, transformational life is righteous
and beautiful in profoundly visible ways! A righteous
and beautiful community may not be easily found in
a church building down the street from where you sit
right now, but make no mistake about it, it exists! It
is not a pink, polka-dotted unicorn. If you've never
tasted it, there are no words I can write to instill in you
how much better and more real it is compared to what
I call "ordinary church." Our churches may or may not
be this Acts 2, awe-filled, red-hot community, but they
are supposed to be.

THE LOCAL CHURCH AND THE RIGHTEOUS AND BEAUTIFUL COMMUNITY

In the next chapter we'll discuss more about what
you can do to actively find and/or create this kind of
community, but for now let me just encourage you to
have hope that it is real and worth pursuing. Many
people in their late twenties to early thirties have given
up on the local church because they know in their

heart of hearts there must be something more. They have a suspicion, a yearning, a desire, and because of that they are insisting on something more. If that is you, your suspicions are right. The church is meant to be better. But don't think that counterfeit church will work.

If we are honest, most of us just don't need the local church to have meaningful community anymore. We can have community online with real people whom we'll rarely, if ever, see in person. Often, people find a closer community in a CrossFit gym, a running club, or yoga class. We see closer glimpses of the righteous and beautiful community in social-justice rallies, online communities, or even down at the local pub than we do at the local church. In none of these places, however, will we find our best selves or our place in God's story. That's not to say these places aren't worth investing in; they just should not become our "core story," the place where our lives and selves unfold. In order for us to truly find our place in the story of everything, we need to be a part of a community of people who are empowered by the Holy Spirit and have a deep conviction about the person and mission of Jesus Christ. That community is the local church, or at least it is supposed to be. The local church is supposed to be the most significant, Spirit-filled, missional community in the life of a person who has come to know and follow Jesus Christ.

So what do we do about finding our way into this

kind of community? If you aren't currently attending a local church, start! I want to challenge you to find a church. Instead of just giving up on the local church or sitting around and complaining about it—do something! Giving up on the local church because a few (or a lot of) people hurt you is like giving up on doctors because one doctor misdiagnosed you. This is too important to let people's mistakes and wrongdoing keep you from living out your place in the story of everything. And you simply cannot live that right, beautiful, and together life apart from the local church. Appendix A has a brief list of suggestions on how to go about finding a local church. If the churches where we live are not the Acts 2 communities they are supposed to be, there are at least three things that we can do. We can move farther out to try to find one that is. We can stay and try to create that kind of community within an existing local church. Or we can be a part of starting a new church. It may surprise you to hear me say that all three are viable ways to pursue having an Acts 2 community.

There is not one easy solution, and the right answer for you and others in your circles depends on many things. I think for the vast majority of people, staying and trying to create this community within your church or a local church is almost always the best first step. Start with gathering people to pray that God would bring deep conviction about sin and mission, that He would fill you with hope, awe, and wonder. Read and study the Bible and share your story with others. Look for things to do together that can create bounty and beauty in your context. Talk about and confess your imperfections—your racism, eating disorders, porn addictions, envy, and other things that are preventing you from knowing and being known by each other and by God. James 5:16 says, "Therefore confess your sins to each other and pray for each other so that you may be healed. The prayer of a righteous person is powerful and effective." The late Steve Hayner, former president of InterVarsity Christian Fellowship, said in response to this Scripture, "When I confess my sins to God, I receive forgiveness. When I confess my sins to a brother in Christ, I receive healing." We need community to grow into who we were meant to be. We need to rejoice and confess, work with and celebrate with others. Community is not just what God tells us to do, it is who God is and what He invites us to, but it does have a cost. The cost is always worth it though. On the other side of the cost of community is our best life and all the incomparable joy of finding our proper place in the story of everything.

CHAPTER 6

DO SOMETHING TOGETHER

"York, let's jump into my new Mercedes and go to lunch." The very first time I met Jim, I was invited to present my ministry with InterVarsity and to ask for financial support. Now, let me say up front that I absolutely love raising money and have been raising money as a full-time employee of InterVarsity Christian Fellowship for more than twenty years. Raising money has taught me more about dependence on God, interdependence on God's people, humility, trust, and celebration than nearly any other part of my Christian life. I've been on hundreds of appointments over the years, so my problem with Jim had nothing to do with the fact that I was depending on his consideration for support; it was Jim himself. He was arrogant, rude, and showy from the moment I met him to the moment I left the appointment.

Sitting down at the restaurant, Jim motioned to the server and said, "We'll both have the Chilean bass and a bottle of sparkling water," and then turning to me said, "Okay, York. What do you have for me?" Jim was obviously used to being in control, directing people and conversations. I actually don't usually have a problem with that either. Many executives of large organizations have the same demeanor as Jim, but he showed a level of self-absorption that made him particularly hard to be around. Two minutes into sharing my ministry with Jim, he said, "That's great, York," and then proceeded to tell me about his recent high-class trip overseas, the house he had built, and more about the car he had and was considering getting rid of because it was not "distinctive enough."

Distinction. It was pretty clear that differentiation, class, and status were super-high values in his mind. The meeting never progressed past stuff that didn't matter. Jim was a man of distinction, a self-made multimillionaire. He was confident, self-reliant, and pretty pleased with himself. From assuming we'd ride together in his car to ordering my meal to taking the entire meeting to tell me about all he had done and achieved, Jim beamed as a shining example of a winner in the American Dream. There is one major problem with the Jims of the world—they are not winners at all.

A vacuum in their lives and a wake of disappointment in their relationships with others both stem from the corruption of the American Dream. This dream weaves self-absorption, arrogance, and self-indulgence into a tangled braid because it tells us that autonomy, self-reliance, and personal success are the ways we get to the winner's circle. There is no place in the American Dream for the biblical value of interdependence, and interdependence (with its core being humility) is at the very core of the story of everything. The path of interdependence is the surest way for you to find your place in the story of everything. Doing something together requires it, so let's look at what it is and what it is not.

OUR DESIRE FOR RIGHT AND BEAUTIFUL THINGS DRAWS US TO OTHERS

Interdependence is vastly different than dependence. In a dependent state, we find ourselves only on the receiving end of a one-way relationship. Dependent relationships are almost always dysfunctional or, by design, intended to be temporary. An infant is entirely dependent on her mother, but we hope that one day she will grow up and become self-sufficient, meeting her own needs to dress, bathe, and eat. An injured athlete in training is dependent on his physical therapist, but the goal is for him to return to the field or arena as a self-sufficient, healthy contributor to his team.

Interdependence is also not the same thing as codependence. Codependence is a label we use for dysfunctional relationships where there is an excessive reliance between people akin to addiction. Weaning off these relational entanglements often feels like a death. One of the ways you can tell the difference between co- and interdependent relationships is that in the former you are never the best version of yourself and neither is the other party. Codependence is at best about surviving, not thriving.

Interdependence is the mature, healthy expression of community. In interdependent relationships and communities, we become the best version of ourselves and we empower others toward the same. Perhaps you've noticed our culture tells us to pursue independence, but this will fail us as it has failed all those who have achieved it. It is interdependence that lies at the very heart of the story of everything. Interdependence is by design in the creation and it is God's intention for us to live into that reality in the church. Paul says it like this in 1 Corinthians 12:4–6: "There are different kinds of gifts, but the same Spirit distributes them. There are different kinds of service, but the same Lord. There are different kinds of working, but in all of them and in everyone it is the same God at work." We were made to thrive in true interdependence.

In fact, all of God's creation is intended to be interdependent. Relationships of interdependence engage in an ongoing mutuality, respect, and love that brings out the best version of the other.

Interdependence is how we live our best life, how we become capable of contributing to the story of everything—it is the way of God's kingdom!

The story of everything from the very beginning to the very end is one of interdependence. This truth is biblical but it is not American. Of the many counterfeits to the story of everything, one of the most powerful is the American Dream. The American Dream places rugged independence, personal wealth, and autonomy on a pedestal. Jim knew this all too well. His life and, in the end, his very identity were based on nothing more than this subtle, easy-to-believe lie. The American Dream says that only losers rely on others, share assets, or voluntarily defer to the needs of those around them. Hasn't there always been something within you that has told you from an early age that this is wrong? Your suspicions are right.

The subtlety of the American Dream allows it to perpetuate itself. Through family trees, communities, denominations, and industries, the American Dream puts forth millions of winners, men and women who are seen as having it done "their way," winning in the end and retiring wealthy and independent. There are many winners in the American Dream, but your suspicions are right—the losers far outweigh the winners. Even in America, this "dream" is quite out of reach for many . . . but the toughest part is that even if you "win" at the American Dream, it still comes up empty.

In the story of everything, one's personal success doesn't come at the expense of the flourishing of others. It takes a lot of work to keep up the lie. The fallacy that the winners tell themselves is that they worked harder for the American Dream. They deserve it. They tell themselves that they buckled down, sacrificed, worked hard, and in the end acquired what they have. While this may be true of some of the winners, most of the ones I know personally are winners not because they worked harder or were smarter than others but because they were born to the right people at the right time and given the right set of opportunities so that with a little work they could get much further than the vast majority of the population. Regardless of that truth, the sad thing is this: in the American Dream the winners aren't winners at all; they just look like winners.

I've met a lot of Jims in my life, and what's most sad about them is that in the end, the bitter end, the American Dream never delivers. Most of the Jims of the world never develop the inner world necessary to belong to others, contribute in meaningful ways to the world around them, or find lasting peace and joy. You see, if we are really going to belong to others, it requires this of us, it's costly.

Without a willingness to live in an interdependent way, we will never be able to experience true community or do something together with others that changes the world around us. You see, in relationships of

*In a community of
healthy, God-centered
interdependence, we
find there always seems
to be more than enough,
an overflow of ideas,
abilities, and energy.*

#dosomethingbeautiful

interdependence, there is more than just an addition of the gifts and abilities of two or more people; there is a multiplication of them. In a community of healthy, God-centered interdependence, we find there always seems to be more than enough, an overflow of ideas, abilities, and energy. Interdependence is how we were designed to function.

Only in the context of community will we ever discover the kind of power we truly need to follow Jesus and do right and beautiful things. As we begin to experience righteousness, our desire for beauty is elevated and we find that we need others more, not less. People who truly influence the world for good are almost never lone-wolf actors, but are men and women embedded in communities with capacity. The plan of God through the church is a dream of beauty and inclusion, of blessing and hope, of righteousness and bounty. The nightmare is that the world chases and perpetuates selfishness, which is, in the end, the fruit of pride. Like beauty, pride accomplishes something. Pride pushes us and the world around us into the nightmare of oppression, exploitation, waste, and self-satisfaction. In my book *Making All Things New: God's Dream for Global Justice*, I say it this way:

> We see the nightmare of our world in the oppression of the weak and marginalized, in the exploitation of natural resources, in crippling diseases and poverty. It lives in brothels where young girls are a commodity, in the brick

kilns where children waste away and in the lost hope of child soldiers. The world we live in is caught in between two worlds—a dream and a nightmare.

But the good news is that that the dream of God will come to pass and is coming to pass all around us.[1]

OUR LONGING FOR COMMUNITY FULFILLS OUR SUSPICIONS

As my first Christian community of interdependence was beginning to disband, I also started my career in marketing and statistical analysis. Each morning I got up, put on a freshly dry-cleaned shirt and tie, and drove thirty minutes to work. My first job was really a dream job. I was hired because of my knowledge of and experience with advanced statistical analysis software through my studies at the University of Michigan. I was making good money for the first time in my life and was moving up in the company.

Each day, however, I ached for something more, to be "on mission" with people, experiencing the Holy Spirit's power and seeing people come to Jesus. It took me a while to realize that my street evangelism days, while very different from a corporate setting, prepared me to share Jesus in my "season of firsts." I had my first real car, my first real romantic relationship, my first real job, and was getting ready to buy my first real house.

Our season of firsts, as I like to call it, can be overwhelming. How can we live passionately for

Jesus while we press into a season of our first real responsibilities? It is a challenging question. Again, part of the answer to this question requires people— we cannot live missionally, passionately, purposefully without people.

My new job made me feel isolated, sitting in a cubicle working on graphs and charts on a computer screen. I longed to be more connected with others, so I began sharing meals during work and after work with my coworkers. The community I had with them was very different from what I had with my Christian friends at church. It didn't take long, however, before I saw how spending time with people really makes an impact. In today's world we can be surrounded by people all day long but never really interact and create meaningful relationships.

The overwhelmingly vast majority of people want relationships. We are wired for it. In fact, your secret longings show you this, don't they? Your suspicions have been true all along. Most likely you experience a great longing for community and you see that same longing in those around you. We were made for the story of everything and that story is about God's love for people.

Making myself available to eat and talk with my coworkers was beginning to have a huge impact on many of them, but it was affecting my life as well. I was mourning the loss of a truly electric group of friends at church and I needed new friends as much as they needed me. The big difference, however, is that in my previous community, Jesus was the absolute center and we all had the Holy Spirit. My relationships with my new coworkers was often tainted with sadness as I saw them self-harm, self-medicate, work in fear, and succumb to a less-than-thriving version of themselves. They needed what my previous community needed: a relationship with Jesus Christ.

During the initial months of forging new relationships at work, I had the opportunity to share Jesus with some hurting and desperate people. Married people were suffering with the infidelity of a spouse. Lonely single people struggled to find friends. Driven people were enslaved to the fear of failure; wealthy people, distracted with the things of this world. Older people were bitter because younger people were passing them by. I began to realize that homeless men on the streets of Detroit had visible needs with visible solutions, but the people in the company I was working at had invisible needs. Meeting those needs was a mixture of the simple and complex. I made myself available and I listened, truly listened. Most people are isolated, and they don't really connect with anyone who will love them by listening to them. But I couldn't just buy them a lunch and sit on the street with them. Their needs were beyond my resources; all I had was my availability and listening ear, but it felt so inadequate compared to what they needed.

GIVING WHAT WE DON'T HAVE

When the needs of people are greater than my resources, I am often reminded of the story of the fish and loaves. Jesus had taught large crowds of people, and as the day ended, a crisis arose:

> By this time it was late in the day, so his disciples came to him. "This is a remote place," they said, "and it's already very late. Send the people away so that they can go to the surrounding countryside and villages and buy themselves something to eat."
>
> But he answered, "You give them something to eat."
>
> They said to him, "That would take more than half a year's wages! Are we to go and spend that much on bread and give it to them to eat?"
>
> "How many loaves do you have?" he asked. "Go and see."
>
> When they found out, they said, "Five—and two fish."
>
> Then Jesus directed them to have all the people sit down in groups on the green grass. So they sat down in groups of hundreds and fifties. Taking the five loaves and the two fish and looking up to heaven, he gave thanks and broke the loaves. Then he gave them to his disciples to distribute to the people. He also divided the two fish among them all. They all ate and were satisfied, and the disciples picked up twelve basketfuls of broken pieces of bread and fish. The number of the men who had eaten was five thousand. (Mark 6:35–44)

Jesus had worked all day, laboring among people who were like sheep without a shepherd. That is how I felt with my coworkers, that they were hurting people without someone to care for them with the right resources. What did I have? Less than five loaves of bread and a couple of fish. In this story, however, Jesus instructs His disciples to order the people, to arrange them for an orchestrated feast. Jesus is about to sound the dinner bell and set the table for thousands of weary souls! What I always find so interesting about this story is the preamble to the feast. Jesus first takes the loaves, blesses them, and then breaks them before they are multiplied.

The multiplication occurs in broken bread, in the torn flesh of a few fish. You see, there is a blessing sandwiched between the taking and breaking that only Jesus could give. The fish and loaves, a small and insignificant amount of resources for thousands to feast on, become all that is needed with the blessing of Jesus. Jesus is able to take and break our resources into something bountiful and beautiful when we give them to Him for blessing. Our resources are never enough to feed the people around us. The great lie of codependency and dependency is that other people are enough. They are not. People are never enough for the feast we were designed for; that can only come from Jesus. Arranging the people in our lives to sit in expectancy for a feast from heaven is an act of faith, but one that is never unmet.

When we get people ready for God's bounty, the blessing of His providence, we are working in interdependence with Jesus Himself. Jesus willingly worked through His disciples. He could have just made fish and bread appear, like the manna from heaven. Instead, the community Jesus is creating models interdependence (He works with us, even though He doesn't need to)! Jesus asked for what food was available. Jesus told the disciples to arrange the people. Jesus asked the disciples to distribute the food and collect what remained.

I too was in a place to share Jesus' bounty. After two years at the company, I had managed to share Jesus with nearly all sixty-five employees. Some had become Christians, some were on their way, and some were seething with anger at me and the other Christians. The few Christians in the company were beginning to band together, to eat together and pray together. A real community of joyful, interdependent people was forming! Our company had two main leaders, one an atheist and one a devout and public Christian. There immediately arose a sharp disagreement between the two of them around religious dialogue and practice in the workplace because of the visibility of our new Christian community.

The practice that rocked the boat the most was the lunchtime Bible study we had in the break room two or three times a week. The Bible study was small but became the catalyst for us to become missional witnesses. As a result of our Bible study, we began thinking about our coworkers differently, praying for them, and working to be good Christian witnesses, particularly now that the heat was on and everyone felt the tension. Something miraculous, however, began to happen. Several of the angriest and most resistant coworkers began to seek me out and to share some of their pain.

One of the most upset coworkers shared privately that her long-term boyfriend had a pornography addiction. Although she had played it off for most of their relationship, accepting it as normal, she now lived in insecurity, fearing that he would leave her for a more attractive, younger woman. Another person told how, because of her age, she envied the new younger workers because she was beginning to realize she would never do much better in the company than what she had accomplished. She was in poor health and was just a few years away from retirement. Another supervisor shared privately that though he supervised multiple departments, all of his direct reports had university degrees. He had never set foot in college. He had worked his way up from the humble beginnings of the firm and feared losing his authority and position to the smart, young college grads like me.

I believe the real reason I got to be a part of these coworkers' confessions and healing was because I loved them by listening. I didn't react by demanding Christian rights in the workplace; I simply made myself available. Like the disciples brought all they had in the loaves and fish and Jesus multiplied it, I brought all I had—my ears and my time—and Jesus did amazing things with it.

One thing I learned along the way was that in many of the cases, the anger of our coworkers had nothing to do with Jesus or Christianity. We had become a collective symbol of largely young, joyful people who were experiencing meaningful relationships and doing well in the company. As the walls began to fall, I felt very much like how I imagine the disciples felt when they picked up the leftovers and found more than they started with. In the aftermath of God's multiplication, you realize Jesus does more, much more, than what was possible with our meager contributions. That is how I felt as my career came to an end at my dream job.

WE LEARN MORE ABOUT WHAT GOD IS LIKE WHEN WE ARE TOGETHER

Interdependence is not a psychological construct manufactured to fuel daytime talk shows, but a biblical idea. The entire Christian doctrine of the Trinity depends on the idea of interdependence. In Genesis 1:26–27 we read,

> Then God said, "Let us make mankind in our image, in our likeness, so that they may rule over the fish in the sea and the birds in the sky, over the livestock and all the wild animals, and over all the creatures that move along the ground."

> So God created mankind in his own image,
> in the image of God he created them;
> male and female he created them.

When God said, "Let *us* make mankind in *our* image,"
He is not referring to anyone else outside of Himself.
This is not a reference to angels. We are not made in
the image of angels, but of God Himself. God is talking
amongst Himself, so to speak, between the three
interdependent persons of the Trinity. The Father,
Son, and Holy Spirit are one in substance and three
interdependent persons. A person in the philosophic
sense is an independent entity with intellect, emotion,
and volition or free will.

In the biblical sense, however, a person is an
interdependent entity, with intellect, emotion, and
volition all intertwined with others in community.
It is a part of the fallen, sinful reality we live in
to experience personhood devoid of community,
something that often leads to a self-destructive
and/or sociopathic end. This is why the story of
everything is so very different than the American
Dream; the latter leads to isolation and death, the
former to joy in the context of community. Even
though we still have individual responsibility, we
were created for community. So when God wanted
to create one organism that would bear His image
and carry His creative authority into the new world,
He did not create a singular organism but rather an
interdependent organism. We see this at the end of

verse 27, again: "So God created mankind in his own image, in the image of God he created *them*; male and female he created *them*." This creative act of "them" is stated two times, with an emphasis that the one organism was not Adam or Eve, but Adam *and* Eve in community. The one organism then that God creates is actually "them," Adam and Eve together. There is a parallel here in God's creation to His essence. In the same way, when Christians say "God," we mean Father, Son, and Holy Spirit—not three gods, but one God existing in three interdependent persons. So when this one God who is three interdependent persons wanted to make one created being to reflect Himself, He does not create Adam or Eve; He creates Adam *and* Eve, who in that communal state reflect God most fully.

The interdependent community Adam and Eve were created to know becomes the living organism that demonstrates the divine stamp of God in creation. This is important because it shows us the interdependence of Jesus on the Father and the Holy Spirit and in each subsequent configuration of the members of the triune Godhead. With this key, we have a much richer understanding of Jesus' prayer in John 17:21–23. As He prepares to go to the cross, to suffer isolation, alienation, and rejection on our behalf, He says,

> "That all of them may be one, Father, just as you are in me and I am in you. May they also be in us so that the world may believe that you have sent me. I have given them the glory

that you gave me, that they may be one as we are one—I in them and you in me—so that they may be brought to complete unity. Then the world will know that you sent me and have loved them even as you have loved me."

God's divine love expands community. The love of God propels the story of everything, enfolding those who belong to Jesus into the very community of God Himself! It is astounding, but the idea of "togetherness" or community is so much more than independent people having mutually beneficial relationships. This is what we were made for, because this is who has made us, our communal, loving God!

DOING SOMETHING TOGETHER IS EASIER SAID THAN DONE

My career at the company was coming to an end just as our new Christian community was coming together. Toward the end of my time, I had begun to develop an assessment of the Detroit area related to college students. I wanted to challenge my church to be more intentional in our efforts to reach the several universities around us. I developed population maps, a budget, even migratory patterns for students living at home in the summer, commuting to nonresidential colleges, and leaving home each fall.

As I presented my grand plan, person after person challenged me to investigate going on staff with InterVarsity USA, a college ministry that was doing phenomenal work in the Detroit area. I was insistent, however, that our church needed to be doing college ministry. I pressed harder and further, getting an audience with deacons and pastors. The meetings always ended the same way, however. "Why don't you just join staff with an organization like InterVarsity?" I was frustrated but still determined. Finally, I got an audience with our missions and outreach pastor, Frank. Frank was a legend, a passionate leader for missions, making a way for the church to do all kinds of amazing things all over the world. This was my big chance. I pulled out all the stops. I hung maps on the wall, presented my budget, made my case.

At the end of it all, Frank took off his glasses, cleaned them off, rubbed his eyes, and looked up at the ceiling for a good while. After thinking, Frank put his glasses back on, looked me in the eye, and asked, "Have you ever just thought about going on staff with some organization, something like InterVarsity?"

I responded in anger, "No, but I guess I better." I packed up and stormed out.

After a few days back in the routine of putting on my dry-cleaned shirts, driving back and forth to the office, and having lunch with my coworkers, my heart began to break as I realized God was calling me out of the corporate world and out of yet another Christian community to join a different one—InterVarsity. After meeting with InterVarsity leaders, I began volunteering, visiting campuses to do evangelism one to two days a week. After a year it was clear that my heart, passion, and gifts really were better used on campus than in the corporate world. Joining other students and staff on campus, I felt alive, with a rush of joy and feelings of awe at what God was doing *in* me and *through* me. Before I knew it, I was embedded in yet another red-hot, Acts 2 community of Christ followers!

I've been on staff with InterVarsity now for more than twenty years, and throughout it all, it has been an electric, awe-filled experience. I have been able to be a part of a true movement of the Holy Spirit on college campuses, and even though I'm now a national leader in the organization, I've committed to preaching the gospel regularly at campuses, conferences, and churches throughout America. I've been humbled to lead thousands and thousands of students to Jesus through my preaching ministry. Each time one comes to faith, as they are added regularly to the church, my heart is filled with joy and thankfulness that I got to have a front-row seat to the love of God!

HOW TO MAKE IT HAPPEN

Doing something together is easier said than done. Joining God in His work and inviting others to join the work also takes time and preparation. It is true that sometimes we "fall into" a community that is doing righteous and beautiful things, but more often, we have to do some work. Understanding where we are, where our home is, where our church has been and is going are all important starting points. One resource that has helped me immensely is John Fuder and Noel Castellanos's work, *A Heart for the Community*. In this resource the authors help us "exegete" our community, analyzing its contours and content with an aim of understanding where the possibilities are. They help us figure out where and how to do the work of righteousness and beauty. In the book they stress the importance of being an "involved participant observer" when entering into the lives of people and communities around us. They say,

> Participant observation is a research method that puts you right in the middle of what or who you are studying.* In this research process, you make no assumptions or judgments; you just observe and listen and learn. You are with the people daily as life is happening.
>
> The difference is that an Involved Christian Participant Observer puts on the flesh of the culture while maintaining a strong belief that "Christ will use me as I do life within this community."[2]

This resource tells us how to go on a treasure hunt for the work of the Spirit, how to enter into what God is doing, and how to bring others along in the work of doing righteousness and beauty.

---

*James P. Spradley, *Participant Observation* (Orlando: Holt, Rinehart and Winston, 1980).

True transformation revolves around righteousness in Jesus Christ, causes the worship that comes out of doing beauty, and results in doing something together for God. The work of God through a righteous and beautiful community should create the fruit we saw in Acts 2. They were all together; they shared things and looked out for one another. They ate and spent time in one another's homes. They were joy-filled, generous, and thankful. This is the result of a community powered by the Spirit, doing the work of Jesus.

DOING SOMETHING TOGETHER EXERCISE

1. Relational Network Map

Take out a large piece of paper and map your relationships. Put yourself at the center and draw a box around your name. Extend as many lines as you need to the names of the meaningful relationships you currently have, regardless of the person's race or ethnicity, religion, financial status, or age. After you list out the names, draw circles around each name. Now, place a star next to the names of the people who give you life, bring out the best in you, celebrate you, and/or empower you. What do they all have in common? Now, place double stars next to the people in your network map that you think need to be empowered, celebrated, or who are not thriving. What do they all have in common? Now, what if you and those single-star people did something together in the double-star lives of those within your relational network? Could you imagine such a thing?

2. Community Network Map

The Acts 2 community of Jesus should also impact the cities and regions in which we live. Do this same exercise for your city or region. Put your church or organization in the box at the center of a large piece of paper. Extend lines to circles that show the single-star people groups, organizations, and places in your community. Things like the local chamber of commerce, organizations that contribute to the overall health of a city, social services, and nonprofits are likely to fill these circles. The single-star elements in our cities and regions give life to the community.

Now, put into circles the double-star entities in your city, the places that need a hand, the places that are desperate for righteousness, the ugly places in need of beauty. I'll bet most of those places have racial, economic, and power disparities in common. These are places where people are trapped in a system that keeps them from the wide variety of good things that we experience in communities with lots of resources. What if you got all the single-star places and people together to do something beautiful with the double-star places? What would that look like? What would happen? My guess is that you would hear and feel a rush of the Spirit, and a miracle of transformation would occur. If done right and in the power of the Spirit, I believe the result would be new communities of empowered, joy-filled, generous people emerging both in the places of need and the places of plenty. What often starts as well-meaning people trying to do good things almost always fizzles out because it lacks real spiritual power. This is why working with others through a relationship map is just a tool to get things started. The real power comes when those who are filled with the Holy Spirit follow Jesus into new and often risky ventures. When that happens, what would have been mere civic responsibility, community activism, or grassroots mobilization can truly become a work of the Spirit.

THE RIGHTEOUS AND BEAUTIFUL COMMUNITY

My colleague Connie and I stared at each other in amazement as we looked out at a packed auditorium at the Ohio State University. For more than a year we had worked together on a weeklong event called the Price of Life, and as it began to unfold we were blown away at the crowds that showed up day after day and night after night. The Price of Life events brought together business leaders, faith communities, nonprofits, medical and legal professionals, community activists, and students to create sustainable solutions in the fight against modern-day slavery.

I've done hundreds of Price of Life events, big and small, all over the United States, but my all-time favorite was the one I did with Connie at Ohio State. On that particular night, the Columbus Barrister Club partnered with us in InterVarsity USA to create a town-hall gathering of political and legal experts to engage the trafficking epidemic in Ohio. At the time, Ohio was struggling badly with sex trafficking, particularly trafficking of the very young, according to their State Attorney General's office.[1] Many came out to the event. Presidents of organizations sat in the front of the auditorium, along with members of the US House of Representatives, federal judges, and local celebrities from every walk of life. The political leaders were there because we asked them to come—to share in our vision of serving the common good. Large crowds of students jammed into the standing-room-only auditorium and listened for hours as speeches were made, questions were asked, and people were celebrated and acknowledged for their work locally, nationally, and globally. Connie and I glanced back and forth throughout the event in amazement.

As amazing as the events of the Price of Life were, what was affecting me so deeply about those at Ohio State was Connie herself. Connie is a relentless worker, an optimist, and someone who can hold her own with the best hard-core sarcasm I can dish out. Since I was a graduate of the University of Michigan, every time I came to town Connie always let me know that I was at *the* Ohio State where wolverines were, in fact, nothing more than animals! Connie was a second-career grandmother who had lived in Columbus most of her life. She was a prayer warrior, Bible studier, gospel sharer, and Jesus lover. I hired her as my campaign director for all these reasons. She came on the team, however, after a very rough start to the campaign.

The Price of Life at Ohio State was almost cancelled after significant problems on the front end with volunteers, employees, and resistance in the community. When we hired Connie to direct the Price of Life, in my heart I knew the campaign would either die or survive based on her ability to pick up the pieces and move us forward. She began strong, assembling leaders from every walk of life, every denomination, business and political leaders, and some of the largest churches in Columbus. They were all coming to the table largely because of Connie's legacy there and her tenacious "woo." To "woo" means to be determined to win someone over to one's side, to establish a sense of connection or bond around a common purpose. Connie was my Price of Life Queen of Woo! Every time I came into town to meet with the leaders Connie had assembled, there would be more people from diverse walks of life and backgrounds because of the Queen of Woo. That is why, when Connie was diagnosed with cancer a few months into the process, my heart sank . . . first for her and second for the campaign. I was sure we were going to have to close shop as Connie began chemotherapy immediately.

VICTORY IN SUFFERING

To my surprise, however, this tenacious Queen of Woo decided that she could, in fact, carry on her campaign director functions while working through the pain and sickness of cancer. At first I didn't believe her, but she won me over too.

The next several weeks were horrendous for Connie. I had a front-row seat to something simultaneously awful and beautiful. I watched her press into purpose, against the pain of cancer medication and therapy, against the challenges of a fragmented coalition, and come out on the other side not just surviving but thriving. It seemed that as Connie suffered physically, she soared in every other way, leading the Price of Life into unprecedented scale and scope! That night, the room was packed with the business, legal, academic, and medical elite. Some of the politicians even flew into town from Washington just for this event. But Connie was the real VIP, the most extraordinary person that night and throughout the week. Whether the tens of thousands of people impacted by the Price of Life that week knew it or not, every single one of them had been influenced personally by this Queen of Woo.

As a follower of Jesus, Connie knew that there was more at stake than just some events. We were trying to do something righteous and beautiful together. We were trying to care for real women and men, trafficking survivors and victims for whom the issue of modern-day slavery wasn't an "issue." It was a real and living nightmare. Throughout the Price of Life events, I have sat, cried, prayed, and mourned with countless individuals who have been personally affected by human trafficking. Mothers who have lost daughters, daughters who were sold by mothers, sons sent to work in luxury hotels against their wills, and fathers sleeping ten deep in warehouse rooms for forced farm labor. Trafficking is not just an issue; it is the greatest humanitarian crisis of our time—even here in America.

At the Ohio State Price of Life, I met one young man who had been sold for sex in Columbus for about two years during his teens. As he joined the events of the week, he said, "What you have done this week is beautiful. It has restored a part of me. Your events are in some of the exact locations where I was forced to wait for my johns. Because of the Price of Life, I have come to believe that what I experienced was evil and that I can find love and restoration even with what has been done to me." Doing something right isn't just a nice-sounding idea; it matters for real people, reverses years of despair, and creates beautiful things in communities.

During the Ohio State Price of Life, through our collaborative effort with hundreds of organizations, we were able to empower state lawmakers in their own ongoing work to fight trafficking. Of particular note was that the energy of the Price of Life played a major part in awakening leaders, students, and citizens to the reality of trafficking and the need to pass new legislation. One brave law student involved in the Price of Life lobbied lawmakers and, as a result, helped pass Ohio's first anti-trafficking bill, State Senate Bill 285. Throughout these campaigns, we influenced individual lives and power structures. We empowered people and institutions. We provided funding and hope, ideas and opportunities. We did all this because we came together as a community, being led by unlikely people like Connie.

AN INVASION FROM ANOTHER WORLD

An invasion is happening all around us. A righteous and beautiful community has emerged. It is here and it is called the church of Jesus Christ! The church has been invading our world since it was born in Acts 2:1–4. There we read,

> When the day of Pentecost came, they were all together in one place. Suddenly a sound like the blowing of a violent wind came from heaven and filled the whole house where they were sitting. They saw what seemed to be tongues of fire that separated and came to rest on each of them. All of them were filled with the Holy Spirit and began to speak in other tongues as the Spirit enabled them.

And then later on in that passage in verses 42–44,

> They devoted themselves to the apostles' teaching and to fellowship, to the breaking of bread and to prayer. Everyone was filled with awe at the many wonders and signs performed by the apostles. All the believers were together and had everything in common.

The church has come, but the church doesn't always look like a building on the corner of some street with a nice sign that says "church." Sure, sometimes it does, but sometimes it looks like a rock concert, a soup kitchen, or an after-school tutoring center. It may look like a simple home caring for foster children or a business providing internships to at-risk teens. Sometimes it can even look like a tenacious Buckeye grandmother struggling with cancer in a room of politicians. The story of everything unfolds through the light of the righteous and beautiful community as it assembles, risks, strives, suffers, and soars. God's people have been doing His otherworldly work in places of brokenness and among broken people ever since that first "sign" of Jesus at the wedding of Cana. It is full of bright light, like a firefly in the night, showing the way of righteousness and beauty in times of darkness.

Individuals themselves are capable of doing extraordinary things, but one of the most powerful, influential things any woman or man can do is to work righteousness and beauty in the context of community. The righteous and beautiful community, the church, is capable of opening a portal in time and space, of doing God's work on earth. Famous missiologist Stanley Hauerwas says of the righteous and beautiful community that it is a "harbinger" from another world, making real the power of God.[2]

Finding our place in the story of everything is about seeing heaven's power, the presence of Jesus, enacted in our lives and our world in a way that enables righteousness and beauty to form in us and through us. Our part in the story of God is always to be a conduit for another time and place, rejoicing as God's power and will infiltrate this world. This can't be done in any sustaining way outside of a community of believers. Individuals do not have the capacity to carry the kind of vision, hope, tenacity, and faith required to truly impact the world. For that, we need each other.

WHEN HEAVEN AND EARTH COLLIDE

You see, heaven and earth collide all the time, and the best part is that they can collide through us when we choose to be vessels of God's desires and power. There is an essential "we" in the invasion of heaven into earth. Consider the Lord's Prayer with the emphasis on community:

> "This, then, is how you should pray: 'Our Father in heaven, hallowed be your name, your kingdom come, your will be done, on earth as it is in heaven. Give *us* today *our* daily bread. And forgive *us* our debts, as *we* also have forgiven *our* debtors. And lead *us* not into temptation, but deliver *us* from the evil one.'" (Matt. 6:9–13)

There is a "we" and an "us" to our relationship with God, His mission and power, our desires and struggles, our debts and need for deliverance. The communal contours of bounty and beauty are baked right in, because we are made in the image of a communal

God. There ultimately can be no beauty or bounty without a community. The righteous and beautiful community is one of the inescapable elements in the story of everything. Although the story is ultimately about God, God has elected to create the story of time and space around community and that includes us, His people, the church!

Theologian N. T. Wright says, "Earthly events . . . are in fact bound up with the heavenly dimension, and thus invested both with a significance which may not appear on the surface and with a clear hope for a future that goes beyond what could be predicted from socio-political observation."[3] In simpler terms, heaven is breaking right in. Heaven is breaking into earth, and while things don't always appear that way, the reality is our actions impact heaven, and heavenly actions impact earth. All of that is what is at stake in the Lord's Prayer, and it is at stake in our choices to be conduits of righteousness and beauty. What Connie did during the Price of Life was to choose to be a conduit for justice and righteousness. A bit of heaven flowed through her body of pain and place of struggle. While I am sure she thought I smiled at her in amazement because of the large crowds and success of the campaign, I really smiled in amazement as I witnessed a bit of heaven on earth through what she allowed herself to be. Connie chose to be a harbinger of the future power of Jesus.

NO MATTER WHO YOU ARE

You can be a harbinger of bounty and beauty too—no matter who you are, what you have, or where you've been. You have a place in the story of God *in spite of* your limitations, fears, and handicaps. You have a place in the story of God *in spite of* struggles and past failures. You have a place in the story of God *in spite of* your lack of knowledge, finances, or other limitations. You have a place in the story of everything *because* God chooses for you to have one. Paul says it like this to the Corinthians:

> But God chose the foolish things of the world to shame the wise; God chose the weak things of the world to shame the strong. God chose the lowly things of this world and the despised things—and the things that are not—to nullify the things that are, so that no one may boast before him. (1 Cor. 1:27–29)

We cannot boast in our part of God's story, but we also can't deny that we have a part—no matter what. Connie's story has been the story of the people of God ever since the story began, but it is breathtaking when you get to see it. It is beautiful to watch someone powerless do something powerful. There's just something really powerful about watching a person with little bounty do bountiful things. Connie's story was possible because God had *chosen* her to do something together with me and others that was beyond herself and *in spite of* herself. This can be your story too.

Now consider the insignificance of a single firefly in the night. Just one firefly against the dense darkness of a summer night might not be appreciated and certainly might be easily missed. It isn't until an entire field or forest flickers green that an extraordinary wonder is born. One person doing righteousness and beauty in the power of the Holy Spirit is almost always missed by the watching world. Many of God's people, however, doing righteousness and beauty are an extraordinary vision, a wonder that challenges our isolation, selfishness, and pain. Connie was great not because she was a tenacious grandmother (and certainly not because she was a Buckeye!). Connie's greatness came because she surrendered herself to Jesus, deciding to be a part of a movement of women and men bent on doing beauty and providing bounty in a dark world.

Consider this same point in reverse. The righteous and beautiful community needs you too. A lot of people doing righteousness and beauty may seem like enough, but there is always room for our contributions. Is that field of magical green light ever really green enough? Every time I see a field of fireflies, as amazing as it is, I always think, "I wish there were more—ten times more!" More. The body of Christ also needs more light, more conduits, more worshipers, more women and men to press through pain and suffering, inadequacies, fear, anxiety, and limitations long enough to light up the night! The righteous and beautiful community needs you and you need it. No matter who you are!

THE FIRST DAY OF THE FOREVER AFTER OF GOD

If there really is a story of everything that God has been weaving since the beginning, where does it all end? Is there a Disneyesque "Happily Ever After"? Yes! In the forever after of God's story, righteousness and beauty come together in a single event. God gathers people groups from every time and place. This single event brings together people speaking sixteenth-century French, unknown languages from undocumented portions of history, and modern-day slang from the south side of Chicago. It welcomes as many hues of skin, colors of hair and eyes, and cultural manifestations as the earth has been able to produce. Singing and dancing, art and music will swirl in such grand, worshipful pageantry as to put the Olympic Games celebrations to shame. In this great event, God's people from all time and space descend as a single body of beauty and bounty. We read of this moment in Revelation 21:1–4:

> Then I saw "a new heaven and a new earth," for the first heaven and the first earth had passed away, and there was no longer any sea. I saw the Holy City, the new Jerusalem, coming down out of heaven from God, prepared as a bride beautifully dressed [other translations use the word *adorned*] for her husband. And I heard a loud voice from the throne saying,

"Look! God's dwelling place is now among the people, and he will dwell with them. They will be his people, and God himself will be with them and be their God. 'He will wipe every tear from their eyes. There will be no more death' or mourning or crying or pain, for the old order of things has passed away."

This is the first day of the forever after of God. God is with His people and they have been "adorned," made right. Blessed with His bounty and beauty.

This passage also tells us that this first day of the forever after of God is a wedding day and Jesus Christ is the groom. All weddings throughout time have merely prefigured this day of days, metaphorically pointing all humanity to this divine moment. We are the bride of Jesus Christ, and on this wedding day Jesus gives us some amazing wedding gifts! He gives us the gift of eternal life, the gift of healing from past pain, and the gift of communal restoration. Most of all, He gives us the gift of Himself. Notice it says that "God's dwelling place" is among people. Through the death and resurrection of Jesus Christ, we are made right with God and will dwell with Him and with one another. This is the ultimate vision for the story of everything. It is where everything is heading.

Notice again the word *adorned*. This is important. The word means so much more than merely being made ready for something fancy. It appears forty times in the New Testament, but almost always in reference to preparation for something historic, official, or special. John the Baptist used the word when he called people to repent and "prepare" the way of the Lord. Jesus used it quite a bit to refer to the adorning necessary to eat at the table of God in the kingdom of heaven. Paul used the word in 1 Corinthians 2:9, "'What no eye has seen, what no ear has heard, and what no human mind has conceived'—the things God has prepared for those who love him." What's most important, however, is that this use in Revelation 21 is the very last time the word is used in the Bible. It is the final preparation, the culmination of all "adorning." The forever after of God begins with us finally being ready to be all we were meant to be, know all we were meant to know, and have all we were meant to have. Because of what Jesus did for us, we are finally ready for God Himself, our true treasure!

BEING IN THE CENTER OF IT ALL

Being in the center of God's will, God's desire for you and for the world, means living into the epicenter of righteousness, beauty, and community. Many of the world's problems, and ours as well, come not from a lack of vision but from an incomplete vision. Having two-thirds of something great may sound good, but when it comes to the story of everything, it is everything or nothing at all. Consider the following partial people and partial communities.

1. *A beautiful community without righteousness:* In this community, there is bounty but perhaps no equality. There is no justice, no access to the things that cause flourishing for all. This community consumes. It is broken in a way that eventually ends in some iteration of hedonism.

2. *A righteous community without beauty:* In this community, there is plenty but no connection to the things that make for a worshipful life. There is no art, no dancing, no sunsets or fireflies. The richness of life is missing. This community follows the rules and gets by. It is broken in a way that eventually ends in legalism.

3. *A righteous person without community:* Here, there is often self-righteousness, the belief that others are to be judged by the standard of oneself. The community for this person is seen as a tool to be used or a nuisance to be avoided. This person typically devolves into hate, fear, isolation, and despair.

4. *A beautiful person without community:* Here, there is often self-indulgence, the posture of self-consumption. The beautiful person is captured by him- or herself and eventually comes to see the community as merely the place where the self is celebrated or even worshiped. This person typically devolves into narcissism.

There are other iterations, but the point is that a partial self or a partial community is not partially good; it is entirely bad. Being all we were meant to be can only happen with God in the nexus of righteousness, beauty, and community.

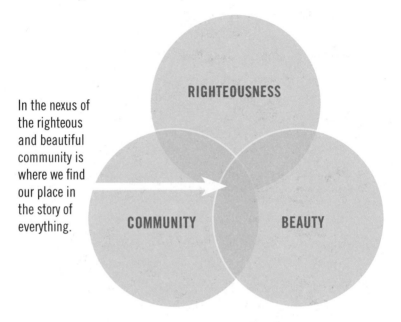

In the nexus of the righteous and beautiful community is where we find our place in the story of everything.

RIGHTEOUSNESS

COMMUNITY

BEAUTY

In Luke 4:18–19 Jesus declares His place in the story of everything by citing a special place from the book of Isaiah. Jesus claims these verses as being fulfilled in Him. He says,

"The Spirit of the Lord is on me,
    because he has anointed me
    to proclaim good news to the poor.
He has sent me to proclaim freedom for the prisoners
    and recovery of sight for the blind,
to set the oppressed free,
    to proclaim the year of the Lord's favor."

We know that Jesus is applying this to Himself when He reads it, but have you ever wondered what comes of those who receive the good news? After Jesus does all this, what happens to those who are set free or recover their sight? What becomes of those who are released from oppression and enter into "the year of the Lord's favor"? In the following verses of Isaiah 61:3b–4 we read the answer:

> They will be called oaks of righteousness,
>   a planting of the LORD
>   for the display of his splendor.
>
> They will rebuild the ancient ruins
>   and restore the places long devastated;
> they will renew the ruined cities
>   that have been devastated for generations.

In these verses we see the very nexus of the righteous and beautiful community. We become a planting of

Salvation: *To be rescued. Within the biblical narrative, to be converted through the work of Jesus Christ on the cross and resurrection to newness of life. Biblical salvation requires a recognition and repentance of one's own sin, a sincere trust in Christ's work on the cross and through His resurrection, a submission to His authority, and commitment to follow Him as Lord.*

the Lord—"oaks of righteousness"! We display His splendor, rebuild ruins, and restore things from devastation. We renew cities and restore lost legacies! This is what grows out of the people who are planted by Jesus' ministry of salvation and restoration: a restoring powerhouse unleashed in the world and in our cities. This is one of the best pictures in all of the Bible that demonstrates what the righteous and beautiful community looks like and where it comes from!

People enter into this nexus through different points. Frequently, people find a wonderful community and there discover what true righteousness and beauty are all about. This was the case in the Price of Life events where thousands and thousands of college students made decisions to become followers of Jesus as a result of participating in the campaigns. They found their way into God's story because they encountered a missional movement of ordinary people like Connie dedicated to providing bounty and beauty in the lives of the needy and vulnerable.

This is largely why, in each campaign I conducted, I always made an effort to partner with non-Christians, even people normally hostile to Jesus and religion. I believe Jesus makes all the difference in the world. I don't believe you need be a follower of Jesus to fight human trafficking, but I do believe you need Jesus to win that fight! In each campaign, we saw many become followers of Jesus because they witnessed the firefly light from another world flicker green as ordinary women and men came together to do beauty and practice righteousness in the area of human trafficking. This works the other way too. If we truly want to transform the world and know ourselves better, we need to work with those who are different, those who are "other," to have the greatest impact.

Christians need non-Christians and non-Christians need Christians in order to really have an impact on our communities, the world, and individual lives. In the context of a community bent on beauty and bounty, I believe the light of Jesus truly shines both in us and through us. Luis Bush, in *The Yes Effect*, says it like this: "If we want to see true transformation in the community we're seeking to help, we need to team up not just with fellow believers, but also with those who don't know Jesus."[4]

Ultimately, what Christians and non-Christians alike need is the bounty and beauty that can only be found in the person of Jesus Christ. In that very nexus of the righteous and beautiful community, we don't find an activity or a campaign. We don't find a church building or program or an event—we find Jesus Christ Himself! Jesus Christ is the center of the story of everything. Knowing Him, following Him, and ultimately being united with Him at the wedding of all time is how we find our best life, how we rightfully rest in our place in the story of everything.

AT THE END OF THE DAY

We sat praying at a table that trembled with the beat of the bass. We were backstage at the New York Price of Life getting ready to speak to a packed auditorium in Times Square. We had done more than one hundred events in the course of a single week, and this was the grand finale. Throughout the week we had partnered with trafficking survivors, including one named Meghan, a beautiful young mom who had been sold for sex in her early twenties. She had agreed to speak at several Price of Life events in New York and later in Michigan. I assumed Meghan was a Christian since we had spoken freely about Jesus throughout all the events and she seemed eagerly agreeable to it all. That's why I was surprised to see her shake and tremble like the walls and table when we asked her to pray. Meghan could not speak and literally shook until I stepped in to pray.

After the event, I flew with Meghan out to the next set of events in Michigan. She and I were to speak to a large crowd assembled in the center of a college campus. I asked her if I could buy her a cup of coffee to warm up before the event. We strolled down to a coffee shop a few blocks down, walking under the fall canopy of wild orange- and red-colored leaves. After getting our coffee, I started, "Meghan, what was going on with you in New York when you trembled backstage?" Meghan, covered with tattoos and piercings, with her vivid, riveting eyes, said surprisingly, "Before that night, I never tied my story as a trafficking survivor to God in any way. It wasn't like I hated God or was angry with God—people did what they did to me, not God." Meghan continued, "The Price of Life in New York started a journey for me. It was the first time I ever thought about what it meant to include God in my story and my work to fight trafficking. Since then, I have started to go to a church, but I'm still not sure what all of it actually means or what it means for someone like me." I was dumbfounded, truly caught off guard but happy to explain what it meant to see God's story through the lens of her story.

I started by saying, "Meghan, first, what you suffered, God suffered. The things that were done to you weren't just painful and unjust to you—they were also painful to God Himself. The Bible tells us that Jesus carries our burdens, He holds our prayers, sees our tears, and is familiar with our pain. Jesus was with you during your times of suffering. Ultimately, Meghan," I continued, "Jesus actually did something to set you free from your literal bondage and all of us from the bondage of evil—He willingly went to the cross where He suffered an unjust death, sacrificing Himself for us." I paused for a moment. "Does this make sense?" I asked.

Meghan responded, "More than you know. Please go on."

I continued, "Meghan, it is important to know that through Jesus Christ, you can be healed and set free. But I want to be honest with you. Evil isn't just something that happened to you, it is also something that is inside of you. You have the same darkness within you that motivated those men to sell you and to use you. The Bible calls this darkness sin. We all have it. None of us are merely victims; we are also all perpetrators." I stopped and sat in silence as I knew I was saying difficult things to Meghan.

She said, "This is putting it all together for me. You don't have to tell me I'm a sinner. I knew that before any of this all happened to me."

I said, "I'm glad to hear you say that, because the rest of the story doesn't make any sense unless we are in agreement on that issue. Meghan, Jesus came back to life after dying on the cross. He is alive and wants to lead your life, to show you life, to give you life. Jesus loves you and wants to cleanse you of the things that have been done to you and by you. He died to do it all. He rose again, and because He is alive, He can lead you into the life you were meant to live. Does this make sense?"

Again, I was blown away by the certitude and clarity of Meghan's response. "This connects all the dots for me in a way I've never been able to see before. This is the missing piece, the next step. I know for sure this is what I want!" We prayed and Meghan asked Jesus to be her leader, she prayed for forgiveness, and most of all, Meghan prayed for God's love and purpose in her life.

As we jogged back to the event that was already underway, Meghan's steps seemed lighter, her face brighter. When she shared her story with the audience, it was clear that she had a light in her that wasn't there in New York. Meghan had been born again—an old-timey phrase but one fitting for a precious daughter who had found meaning, purpose, and hope in the person of Jesus Christ.

This is the righteous and beautiful community at its best. Fighting trafficking and freeing survivors; mobilizing tens of thousands; fostering children; alleviating poverty; changing laws; raising money; creating new worshipers; releasing women from oppression; preaching the gospel; teaching the Bible; trembling in prayer. The righteous and beautiful community is all of these things and so much more. It may or may not always happen in a church building. It may be a backstage table or a coffee bar. It may or may not happen in a pulpit. It may be under the canopy of fall leaves on a college campus. The righteous and beautiful community unfolds where women and men choose to allow Jesus Christ to have His way, to adorn them with bounty and beauty and use them powerfully in a place of need and want. It is in that nexus where we find Jesus. Stooping down to care for a sick woman, to raise a child, to recognize the sick, and to call all us daughters and sons back to the table, to get it while it is hot!

Your place in the story of everything begins and ends with Jesus. Have you made the same decision for Him that Meghan did? Finding that place requires a righteousness that comes only through the beauty of community—first community with Jesus and then community with others who also follow Jesus. As we end, consider a final time praying this prayer from chapter 1:

> God, I want to be made right with You. I want to know You. I acknowledge that Jesus paid the debt for all that I've done and not done, and I receive the gift of His death in my place. I ask that You cure me from the infection of sin through the medicine of the blood of Jesus. Come into my life and lead me. I want You to be the Lord, the leader, of my life. Thank You for welcoming me into Your kingdom! I believe You are alive, Jesus. I believe You were raised from the dead, and I'm asking You to forgive me and include me at the dinner table You have prepared.

FINDING A LOCAL CHURCH

1. Instead of trying to find a church with *perfect people*, look for an honest church where people are dealing with their issues. Evangelist Erwin McManus says,

> The Christian community is not a place without interpersonal crisis or challenge. In some sense we are all hypocrites in transition. We're all working it out. Sometimes fighting with God; sometimes working with God. That's why biblical community is such an extraordinary gift. It's not about being perfect or loving people who are always easy to love; it's about loving people through the love of God. It's about being loved even when you blow it, being loved even when you do not deserve it, and being loved by others who know you all too well—even when you find it difficult to love yourself.[1]

2. Instead of trying to find a *comfortable* church, go on a hunt for where the Spirit is present and actively at work. You can usually spot this because where the Holy Spirit is, we always find things like awe, joy, gladness, generosity, and self-sacrifice. Where you find people looking up at the beauty of Jesus, people who aren't afraid to weep and gasp with laughter, there you will find the makings of a real Acts 2 community.

3. Instead of trying to find a *culturally relevant or cool* local church, go on a hunt for authenticity. Instead of looking at Google ratings of local churches where you are greeted within the first five minutes of entering the building or where you can check your child into a class or nursery effortlessly with a computerized kiosk, go looking for a place that's full of awe, joy, gladness, generosity, and self-sacrifice.

4. Instead of trying to find merely an *inspirational* church, insist on a truthful church. The most important thing to look for in a church is a commitment to the Bible. Without that, everything else falls apart. A good church ought to preach the gospel, be centered on the Bible, have a good grasp on theology, and demonstrate all this with a humble posture of prayer. We cannot know the story of everything or ever find our place in it without the Bible, and if a church is not committed to the Bible, it will never be the righteous and beautiful community it was intended to be.

DEFINITIONS OF WORDS USED THROUGHOUT THE TEXT

BEAUTY: Manifest expressions of either naturally occurring or constructed elements of our experienced reality that elicit some emotional, physical, and/or mental pleasure.

BOUNTY: A wide variety of good things given freely and in large amounts.

COMMUNITY: Peoples meaningfully connected to one another because of a common experience, set of ideals or vision, and/or hope for the future.

EMBRACE: The act of holding something or someone in a way that demonstrates love, compassion, acceptance, and the value of that which is being held.

MERCY: To give or receive that which is not deserved; to express or receive condescension without the expectation of recompense and not on the basis of merit.

RIGHTEOUSNESS: The state of being made morally acceptable to God.

RISK: The state of being exposed to uncertainty and, by extension, certain dangers associated with such uncertainty.

SACRIFICE: To surrender or give up something for the sake of another person, on behalf of an ideal or commitment, or to attain a greater benefit.

SALVATION: To be rescued. Within the biblical narrative, to be converted through the work of Jesus Christ on the cross and resurrection to newness of life. Biblical salvation requires a recognition and repentance of one's own sin, a sincere trust in Christ's work on the cross and through His resurrection, a submission to His authority, and commitment to follow Him as Lord.

ACKNOWLEDGMENTS

Big thanks to the Moody team, particularly Duane and Randall. Thanks, Duane, for having that Diet Coke with me in Orlando! That "back of the napkin" discussion sparked the conversation that has become *Do Something Beautiful*! Thanks, Randall, for pressing the ideas of a couple of dreamers into something concrete and bringing the best out of my thoughts and convictions! Thanks to my friends and colleagues who endure my strange ramblings about another world. I know at times I appear out of my mind as I obsess about what could be in a world of what is. Thanks to my wife, Jodi, for loving who I am and not who I should be. Thanks to Kiren, my only son, for your friendship and love of the world. Thanks to my precious Addison—your love of beauty and your commitment to God's mission inspire me. Thanks to my passionate daughter Gabby—your love for people challenges me to be a better person!

NOTES

INTRODUCTION

1. C. S. Lewis, *Till We Have Faces* (San Diego: Harcourt Brace Jovanovich, 1956), 74.
2. Scot McKnight, *The Heaven Promise: Engaging the Bible's Truth about Life to Come* (New York: Crown Publishing Group, 2016), 78.

CHAPTER 1: A WORLD MADE RIGHT

1. Stanley Hauerwas, *A Community of Character: Toward a Constructive Christian Social Ethic* (Notre Dame, IN: University of Notre Dame Press, 1981), 15.
2. R. York Moore, *Making All Things New: God's Dream for Global Justice* (Downers Grove, IL: InterVarsity Press, 2012), 61.

CHAPTER 2: DO SOMETHING RIGHT

1. Timothy J. Keller, *Making Sense of God: An Invitation to the Skeptical* (New York: Viking, 2016), 147.
2. Noel Castellanos, *Where the Cross Meets the Street: What Happens to the Neighborhood When God Is at the Center* (Downers Grove, IL: InterVarsity Press, 2015).

CHAPTER 3: A WORLD MADE BEAUTIFUL

1. Makoto Fujimura, *Culture Care: Reconnecting with Beauty for Our Common Life* (Downers Grove, IL: InterVarsity Press, 2017), 51.
2. Patrick T. McCormick, *God's Beauty: A Call to Justice* (Collegeville, MN: Liturgical Press, 2012), 30.
3. Ibid., 71.
4. J. D. Douglas, *The New Bible Dictionary*, 1st ed. (Grand Rapids: Eerdmans, 1962), 107.
5. Louie Giglio, *I Am Not But I Know I Am: Welcome to the Story of God* (New York: Crown Publishing Group, 2009), 145–46.

6. R. York Moore, *Growing Your Faith by Giving It Away: Telling the Gospel Story with Grace and Passion* (Downers Grove, IL: InterVarsity Press, 2005).

CHAPTER 4: DO SOMETHING BEAUTIFUL

1. Dallas Willard, *The Divine Conspiracy: Rediscovering Our Hidden Life in God* (San Francisco: HarperSanFrancisco, 1998), 342.
2. Timothy J. Keller, *The Reason for God: Belief in an Age of Skepticism* (New York: Dutton, 2008), 95.

CHAPTER 5: A WORLD BROUGHT TOGETHER

1. Cornelius Plantinga Jr., *Not the Way It's Supposed to Be: A Breviary of Sin* (Grand Rapids: Eerdmans, 1996), 98.
2. Ibid., 14.

CHAPTER 6: DO SOMETHING TOGETHER

1. R. York Moore, *Making All Things New: God's Dream for Global Justice* (Downers Grove, IL: InterVarsity Press, 2012), 11–12.
2. John Fuder and Noel Castellanos, *A Heart for the Community: New Models for Urban and Suburban Ministry* (Chicago: Moody, 2009), 169.

CONCLUSION: THE RIGHTEOUS AND BEAUTIFUL COMMUNITY

1. "2009 Ohio Attorney General's Office Annual Report," Scribd, https://www.scribd.com/document/28927990/2009-Ohio-Attorney-General-s-Office-Annual-Report.
2. Stanley Hauerwas, *A Community of Character: Toward a Constructive Christian Social Ethic* (Notre Dame, IN: University of Notre Dame Press, 1981), 498.
3. N. T. Wright, *The New Testament and the People of God* (London: SPCK, 1992), 290.
4. Luis Bush, *The Yes Effect: Accepting God's Invitation to Transform the World Around You* (Chicago: Moody, 2017), 105.

APPENDIX A: FINDING A LOCAL CHURCH

1. Erwin Raphael McManus, *An Unstoppable Force: Daring to Become the Church God Had in Mind* (Colorado Springs: David C. Cook, 2013), 267.

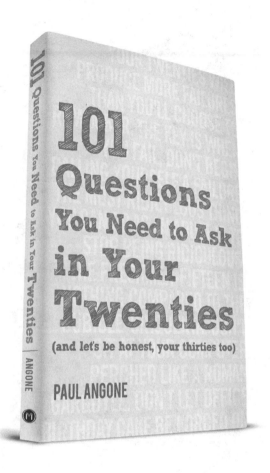

BECOMING A PERSON OF GODLY COURAGE IN A SINFUL WORLD

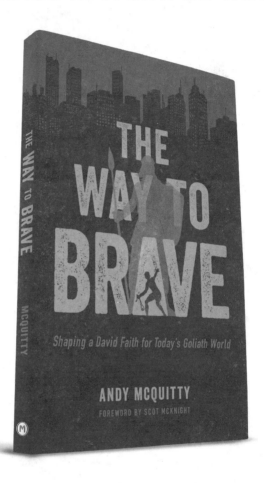

The Way to Brave guides you along the pathway to a courageous soul. Andy McQuitty looks at the life of David and the five key phases God takes all servant leaders through. He'll teach you how to embrace God's work in your own life so that when your Goliath moment comes, you'll be equipped to stand, fight, and win.

978-0-8024-1807-4 | also available as an eBook